tumbling and balancing

tumbling
and balancing

BASIC SKILLS AND VARIATIONS

Judith M. Gedney
Western Illinois University

KLINCK MEMORIAL LIBRARY
Concordia Teachers College
River Forest, Illinois 60305

PRENTICE-HALL, INC., *Englewood Cliffs, New Jersey 07632*

Library of Congress Cataloging in Publication Data

GEDNEY, JUDITH M   (date)
   Tumbling and balancing.

   Includes index.
   1. Tumbling. I. Title.
GV545.G42   796.4'7   76-39945
ISBN 0-13-932798-3

© 1977 by Prentice-Hall, Inc., Englewood Cliffs, N.J. 07632
*All rights reserved. No part of this book
may be reproduced in any form or by any means
without permission in writing from the publisher.*

Printed in the United States of America

10   9   8   7   6   5   4   3   2   1

PRENTICE-HALL INTERNATIONAL, INC., *London*
PRENTICE-HALL OF AUSTRALIA PTY. LIMITED, *Sydney*
PRENTICE-HALL OF CANADA, LTD., *Toronto*
PRENTICE-HALL OF INDIA PRIVATE LIMITED, *New Delhi*
PRENTICE-HALL OF JAPAN, INC., *Tokyo*
PRENTICE-HALL OF SOUTHEAST ASIA PTE. LTD., *Singapore*
WHITEHALL BOOKS LIMITED, *Wellington, New Zealand*

The author wishes to extend a warm thank-you
to all who have helped make this book possible:

> *family members*
> *students*
> *teachers*
> *friends*

and especially to Mrs. Lillian Schneider,
who was patient enough to teach a clumsy little kid to tumble.

contents

preface	*xiii*
notes to the reader	*1*
Use of Progressions to Improve the Learning Situation	*2*
Selection of Spotting Techniques	*3*
Selection of Variations of the Basic Skills	*3*
Suggestions from the Author	*4*
Terminology	*6*
chapter 1 rolls	*7*
Forward Roll Progressions	*7*
Pike Forward Roll to Stand	*9*
Forward Roll to Supine Position	*10*

Forward Roll to Knee Scale	*12*
Forward Roll to Half Split	*13*
Forward Straddle Roll	*14*
Forward Roll One-Quarter Turn to Split	*16*
Forward Roll to Split	*16*
Forward Roll One-Quarter Turn to Kneeling Position	*17*
Forward Roll to Kneeling Lunge Position	*18*
Forward Roll to Lunge	*19*
Forward Roll to Jump	*20*
Forward Roll to a Body Wave	*21*
Forward Roll Without Hands	*22*
Forward Straddle Roll Without Hands	*23*
Forward Roll into Handstand Balance	*23*
Diving Forward Roll	*25*
Forward Roll to Knee Spin	*25*
Kick-Back Forward Roll	*26*
Backward Roll Progressions	*27*
Backward Roll	*29*
Backward Roll to Knee Scale	*29*
Backward Roll to Both Knees	*31*
Backward Roll to Prone Position	*32*
Backward Roll to Lunge	*33*
Backward Straddle Roll	*33*
Backward Pike Roll	*35*
Backward Roll to Headstand	*35*
Backward Roll to Forearm Stand	*37*
Backward Roll to Handstand (Back Extended Roll)	*37*
Backward Roll to a Wide Arm Handstand	*39*
Backward Roll Without Hands	*40*
Backward Roll to Chest Stand	*40*
Tuck Position Side Roll	*41*
Forward Shoulder Roll	*42*
Backward Shoulder Roll	*43*
Additional Forward Roll Variations	*44*
Additional Backward Roll Variations	*47*
Additional Side/Shoulder Roll Variations	*49*

chapter 2   inverted balances   51

Tri-Pod Balance	51
Tip-Up Balance	53
Extended Tri-Pod Balance	53
Headstand Balance	55
Forearm Balance (Elbow Stand)	58
Handstand	62
Handstand Poses	64
Variations Moving out of the Handstand Balance	65
Variations into the Handstand Position	68
Additional Inverted Balance Variations	70

chapter 3   back bends   73

Back Bend Progressions	73
Walking in the Back Bend Position	77
Pony Kicks	78
Inside-Outs	78
Front Limber	79
Forward Walkover	83
Control Forward Walkovers	85
Forward Kick Walkover	86
Forward Double Kick Walkover	87
Forward Cabriole Walkover	87
Forward Scissor Walkover	88
Partner Forward Walkovers	89
Forward Walkover to Split Position	90
One-Arm Walkover	91
One-Arm Control Walkovers	92
Forward Walkover on Cane or Baton	93
One-Arm Partner Walkovers	93
Chasing Walkovers	94
Spotting Forward Walkovers	95
Backward Kickover	96
Backward Walkover	96

Backward Walkover to a Swedish Fall Position 98
Control Backward Walkover 99
Backward Kick Walkover 100
Backward Double Kick Walkover 101
Backward Cabriole Walkover 101
Backward Scissors Walkover 102
One-Arm Backward Walkover 103
Backward Walkover on Cane or Baton 104
Spotting Backward Walkovers 104
Gaining Backward Walkovers 105
Swing-Through Backward Walkover 106
Partner Walkovers 107
Backward Walkover to Split 107
Backward Walkover to Handstand Balance 108
Half Turning Backward Walkover 109
Full Turning Backward Walkover 110
Backward Arabian Limber 111
Veldez Progression 112
Additional Back Bend Variations 117

chapter 4 cartwheels 119

Cartwheel Progression 119
Continuous Cartwheels 120
Continuous Cartwheels Alternating Left and Right Sides 121
Cartwheel to Inward Lunge 122
Cartwheel to Outward Lunge 123
Cartwheel with Hands Held Together 123
Cartwheel Full Pivot to Back Roll 124
Control Cartwheel 125
Control Cartwheel Using Scale Position 125
Control Cartwheels Using Scale Position Progressing Down Length of Mat 126
Near Arm Cartwheel 127
Far Arm Cartwheel 128
Cabriole Cartwheel 128
European Tumbling Skip into Cartwheel 129
Diving Cartwheel 130

Cartwheel to Kneeling Position	*131*
Cartwheel to Kneeling Position on Near Leg	*132*
Cartwheel from Kneeling Position on Far Knee	*134*
Cartwheel from Kneeling Position on Near Knee	*134*
Round-Off	*135*
Switch Leg Cartwheel	*136*
Swing-Through Cartwheel	*137*
Quarter Turning Cartwheel	*138*
Cartwheel to Split	*139*
Partner One-Arm Cartwheels	*140*
Cartwheel on Cane or Baton	*141*
Half Turning Cartwheels	*141*
Running Quarter Turning Cartwheel	*142*
Butterfly	*142*
Forward Tinsica	*143*
Backward Tinsica	*144*
Backward Tinsica with One-Quarter Turn	*145*
Additional Cartwheel Variations	*147*

chapter 5 springs **149**

Knip-up Progression	*149*
Knip-up	*150*
Headspring Progression	*151*
Headspring	*152*
Forward Handspring Progression	*155*
Forward Handspring	*155*
Backward Handspring Progression	*157*
Lean-Back Backward Handspring	*159*
Backward Handspring from Handstand Snap-Down	*160*
Sit-Back, Back Handspring Progression	*162*
Sit-Back, Back Handspring	*163*
Backward Handspring Variations	*163*
Additional Spring Variations	*165*

index **167**

preface

Youngsters of all ages usually enjoy participating in tumbling skills that are geared to their capabilities. This self-testing activity is ego-enhancing when the participants experience success in executing the many possible variations of basic tumbling skills. Consider some of the many advantages of a tumbling unit in the physical education curriculum. Tumbling is a year-round, all-weather activity that lends itself to group instruction and requires a minimum of special equipment. The activity may be taught in either large or small areas. Tumbling experiences may develop not only the student's motor skills but also flexibility; muscular strength and endurance; static and dynamic balance; coordination; control of the center of gravity; agility; rhythmic skill; timing; confidence; and a keen kinesthetic awareness. Tumbling is the one activity that is basic to all events in the area of gymnastics. Through participation in tumbling skills, students have an opportunity to experiment with and develop their creativity.

A combination of these advantages and outcomes of the tumbling unit makes it a valuable part of the physical education program. Yet, it is interesting to note that many elementary and secondary schools either do not include tumbling in their programs, or they offer a very limited skill selection within the unit. One reason may be that in their professional preparation many physical educators received little or no formal tumbling instruction. The typical methods class in gymnastics involves working with a small class of highly skilled and easily motivated fellow physical education majors. The inadequacy of this training becomes apparent when the teacher faces large classes where many of the students have never experienced a forward roll, where some may be apathetic, and only a few will be well skilled and easily motivated. In short, it is the reverse of the simulated teaching situation experienced in college. In order to improve the situation the physical educator turns to resource materials to expand tumbling knowledge.

Tumbling skills basic to all gymnastic events are discussed in many books, but usually such discussion is brief and inadequate. Particularly lacking is information concerning basic tumbling skills, the many variations of these basic skills, spotting techniques necessary to assist the learner, and possible skill progressions to help eliminate anticipated difficulties in executing the skill successfully. It would appear that the elimination of this material from many of the books is because the authors endeavor to cover the entire field of gymnastics in one publication. Because of the constant increase in the number of gymnastic skills a complete book of gymnastics is virtually impossible.

Because tumbling is the one element involved in all gymnastic events, the writer feels that a strong foundation in this area would carry over and improve the learning situation when students are involved in apparatus work. If physical education instructors were well versed in teaching tumbling, students would learn good techniques as well as develop control of the body, kinesthetic awareness, and confidence in experimenting with their creativity. Development of these important qualities during a tumbling experience, when the students are close to the ground and on a mat rather than high above the mat on a piece of equipment, leads to a safer apparatus situation and hastens the learning process.

The purpose of this book, then, is to aid the physical educator involved in teaching a tumbling unit. The book includes explanations of the basic skills and descriptions of teaching progressions and spotting techniques for each skill. Unique variations to the basic skills are described, which give the beginning or intermediate student incentive to experiment with his or her individual creativity.

This book is divided into six chapters—"Notes to the Reader" and five others. "Notes to the Reader" includes an explanation of the intended use of this book and explains the rationale behind the use of the basic tumbling skills; use of teaching progressions, spotting techniques, and variations; and tells how to encourage the student to express his or her creativity.

Chapter 1 is divided into three parts: forward rolls, backward rolls, and side and shoulder rolls. This chapter includes explanations of the basic skills, teaching progressions for these skills, and appropriate spotting techniques. All the variations to the rolls are included.

Chapter 2 deals with progressions, spotting techniques, and variations to the inverted balance skills.

Chapter 3 includes all the material pertaining to the basic skill known as the back bend.

Chapter 4 contains material, progressions and variations, pertaining to the cartwheel.

Material pertaining to the spring category is included in Chapter 5.

J. M. G.

Macomb, Illinois

tumbling and balancing

notes to the reader

This book about basic tumbling is designed to be of assistance to the teacher of tumbling skills and includes explanations of basic skills, sequence stick figures of the skill, descriptions of good technique execution, teaching progressions, and spotting techniques as well as creative beginning and intermediate level variations to each skill.

An analysis of various complex tumbling skills indicated that these complex skills could be broken down into component parts: simpler skills. The resulting component parts were categorized into types of basic tumbling skills. Through this categorization, five basic tumbling skills were discovered: rolls (spine in a flexed position, rotation about the frontal axis); inverted balances (spine extended); cartwheels (spine extended rotation about the sagital axis); back bends (spine hyperextended, rotation about the frontal axis); and springs (spine somewhat extended, rotation about the frontal axis, and the body momentarily suspended in the air). The format of this book has been set up according to this skills classification. Each of the five chapters is devoted to progressions, skill explanations, diagrammatic examples of the skill, spotting techniques, teaching cues, and variations of the basic skill in question.

USE OF PROGRESSIONS TO IMPROVE THE LEARNING SITUATION

The author has had an opportunity to teach tumbling skills to a variety of ability levels for many years. As the classes increased in size and in ability levels, it became difficult merely to present an entire skill to the class and through spotting techniques expect all students to learn within similar time periods. Students with previous experience in executing these activities seemed to learn relatively quickly; students without this valuable previous experience were often found to be much slower; and students lacking in strength, flexibility, and/or timing experienced many difficulties in learning. In order to avoid wasting valuable class time in manually assisting many students through a skill, a part–whole method of presenting the tumbling skills was devised. The author has separated many of the tumbling skills into component parts. Each part of the total skill can be used as an exercise during the warm-up period. If the students practice the various parts of a skill before attempting the entire skill, it is anticipated that they all would gain the kinesthetic awareness of that skill. In short, all students would gain the previous experience so valuable in improving the learning situation. Through verbal cuing by a knowlegeable instructor during these exercise periods, students could learn the necessary timing of the force applications and absorptions. The author refers to these exercises as *progressions*. Progressions can be made up for any tumbling skill. They can be used to give the student the feeling of parts of the total skill that they are about to learn or they can be used as exercises to increase strength, flexibility, and/or timing specifically for that particular skill. When used in the tumbling class situation, progressions allow the instructor to notice the student's problem areas and afford an opportunity for the correction of these problems before it becomes necessary to single out individual students by manually assisting them through the skill.

SELECTION OF SPOTTING TECHNIQUES

Spotting techniques described in this book are designed to control the students' movements in an effective and mechanically efficient manner. Attention is given to controlling the subject's center of gravity as well as to protecting the head and neck area to insure the safety of the student. The methods are *not* designed to execute the entire skill for the subject; this process does little to develop the student's kinesthetic awareness. The spotting techniques have been tested and revised over a period of time and have been found to be most helpful by the author.

SELECTION OF VARIATIONS OF THE BASIC SKILLS

Presentation of only the well-known basic tumbling skills or the inclusion of only a small number of variations leads to boredom for the students. This often used procedure tends to stifle the student's desire to experiment with movement and to be creative. When the teacher is prepared with a large number of variations for each basic skill, the tumbling class can become more interesting and more challenging for each student. The variations of the basic skills presented here are designed to challenge the abilities of all students. A large selection of skills are presented that are within the capabilities of the very beginning student. Unique variations are presented for the highly skilled student. The variations selected were chosen to develop complete control of the student's body. They were purposely designed to move the subject through different planes, different levels, and different directions using different rhythm patterns of movement. An effort was made to develop the student's coordination of both the dominant and the nondominant body segments.

notes to the reader

Blank pages are included at the end of each chapter of the book in order to afford the reader with the opportunity to add to the text any unique variations.

SUGGESTIONS FROM THE AUTHOR

Teach the students the basic skills so that they learn to move safely and use good form and technique. Teach several variations of the basic moves so that the students can experience controlling their bodies through a variety of positions. Then encourage the students to create their own unique variations of the basic skills. This can be done by incorporating the following with each of the basic skills: static poses; basic dance steps and turns; flexibility exercises; any conditioning exercises; stretches and contractions and level changes. Beginners tend to mimic the movements of others. As they gain confidence in their body control and in their self-image, they become more creative. Since these students are potential teachers, it is important that their efforts in dabbling in creativity be encouraged.

Do not be tempted to teach an entire lesson of rolls as found in the first chapter of the book. This book is not set up in lesson plan form. The author suggests that the lesson plan include selected variations and progressions from several of the five basic skills. Spending an entire period on rolling activities tends to lead to sore and stiff neck muscles as well as dizziness for the novice. Avoid this by presenting some roll variations along with cartwheels and back bends or with balances and progressions for springs.

Present the progression to the desired skill a day or two (depending on the difficulty of the skill) before giving instruction in the entire skill. Be flexible in outlining the skill selection for your daily lesson plan. If it becomes clear during the progressions and warm-up exercises that the majority of the students cannot execute the lead-up skill successfully, postpone the more advanced variations for a later lesson.

Be very watchful during the progression practice or warm-up exercise period. It saves time to notice which students have difficulties with body positions, control, and timing of the skill. It is also interesting to notice the students who have perceptual problems; identify them quickly and prepare lesson plans that will give them a feeling of success rather than icluding only skills that they are not capable of completing at the time.

After several class activity periods, group your students according to their abilities if possible. Ability grouping makes it possible for the beginners to concentrate on variations of the basic skills that involve little difficulty while the more advanced students are not bored or at a standstill but are instead working on variations with a higher degree of difficulty. A relatively fast method of ability grouping is to assign the students to groups according to how well they can execute continuous cartwheels on the dominant side and the nondominant side and how well they can go down into and stand up out of a back bend position. Students with strength, flexibility, coordination, and timing can do these skills reasonably well. The novice might have trouble pushing up into a back bend position and encounter difficulties in performing the cartwheel to either side.

Make the tumbling class a thinking class. During part of the lesson, plan to present skills with predetermined directional changes. Tell the students to move down the length of the mat doing a forward roll to a right knee scale, a roll to a left knee scale; a roll to a knee scale straight ahead, and then repeat the series. Such a plan requires that the students think. Beginners often think that doing a skill very fast is doing it well. Insist that they move in a controlled manner and require them to think about what their body parts are doing. Since students forget to think about what they are doing, it is important to talk to them during their work. Verbal reinforcement is very necessary in this self-testing activity. Try to reassure the students and to give constructive criticisms in a positive manner. Once the student is successful in doing a skill, offer a new challenge by encouraging the student to show total amplitude (range of motion) while doing the skill and also demonstrating total control.

As your students discover new and different variations of the skills, it would be wise to jot them down in the appropriate chapter. Since it is always difficult to remember some of the variations, save time by getting them in writing.

TERMINOLOGY

St. Pos.: Starting position for that skill.

Sk. Init.: Skill initiation. The technique the student uses to initiate the movement of the skill.

Recovery: The movement the student makes in order to return to the standing position after executing the skill.

Spotting: Directions given to the teacher in order to assist the performer manually in executing the skill.

Near Arm: Arm closest to the body or the arm that is used first in executing the skill.

Far Arm: Arm that is away from the body or the second arm that would be used in executing the skill.

L.: Left.

R.: Right.

1
rolls

FORWARD ROLL PROGRESSIONS

Tuck Position Roll-Ups

St. Pos.: Sit in the tuck position with the hands grasping the shins and pull the knees tightly to the chest. Tuck the head so that the chin touches the chest and the back is completely rounded.

Sk. Init.: Keeping the chin to the chest, roll backward to the shoulders. Then return to the seated tuck position by pulling the knees to the chest. Repeat several times. Reminder: Each vertebra should contact the mat smoothly and gently. Students whose lower back muscles are tight will fall onto their backs, roll onto the shoulders, and then on the return to the starting position will fall onto the hips. Lower back stretching exercises should be used to correct this problem.

Variation: From the above tucked position roll onto the shoulders so that the head contacts the mat *while* the chin is on the chest; return through the squat position onto the feet by pulling the knees to the chest (this pulling action positions the feet under the center of gravity and the student can stand); as the feet contact the mat, reach forward with the arms and stand up. Repeat several times. Reminder: Legs remain pressed together during the entire progression.

Pike Position Push-Up

This is an arm/shoulder strengthening exercise that is specifically designed to simulate the pushing action needed to successfully complete the controlled forward and backward rolls.

St. Pos.: Stand with the legs together and straight. Place the hands on the mat approximately 24" ahead of the feet. Keep hips high. Hold the head so that the focus is on the mat area directly between the hands (a).

Sk. Init.: Slowly lower the forehead to the mat (b); then return to the starting piked position (a) by pressing with the arms and forcing the hips backward and upward over the feet. Repeat this push-up and work up to five repetitions. Learn to thrust the hips backward and upward to return to the starting piked position. This gives the kinesthetic awareness of doing the skill by controlling the center of gravity rather than by using arm strength alone as in (c) and (d).

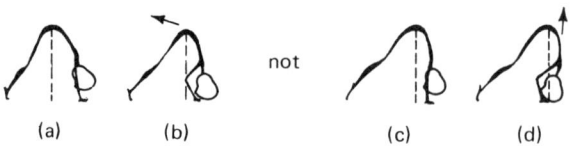

(a)   (b)   not   (c)   (d)

rolls

Variation: Assume the piked push-up position with the head tucked so that the chin contacts the chest (e). Lower the back of the head gently to the mat (f) and return to the starting position (e) by pushing off the mat with the arms and head while moving the hips backward and upward over the feet. Repeat and work up to five repetitions.

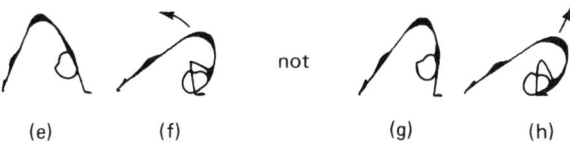

(e)   (f)   not   (g)   (h)

By combining the variations of the two above progressions, the students will be able to execute a slow and controlled forward roll. This skill is explained next.

PIKE FORWARD ROLL TO STAND

Progression: See the explanation for the forward roll progression.

St. Pos.: Piked push-up position with the chin tucked to the chest (a).

Sk. Init.: Slowly lower the back of the head to the mat (b). As the head contacts the mat, press off the mat with the feet by pointing the toes; this ankle extension moves the hips overhead in a controlled manner (jumping off the feet is not necessary). Roll smoothly along spine while maintaining a *tight pike* position; keep legs straight (c).

Recovery: Roll to a V-sit position (d); flex the knees to lower the feet to the mat; reach arms forward to assist in assuming the standing position (e and f).

Spotting: During the pike position kneel to the side of the student's shoulders. Place one hand on the back of the head close to the neck; place the other hand on the back of the mid-thigh area. Have the student tuck the chin to the chest and slowly bend the elbows; you can control tucking the head if necessary and be able to lower the student slowly to the mat making contact on the back of the shoulders. Your hand on the thigh controls the position of the center of gravity; as the head contacts the mat, assist in pulling the hips over the head. As the roll continues down the spine, release the thigh area but maintain the hand position on the head. With your hand still on the student's head, you are able to assist in pushing and lifting the student into an erect standing position.

Tips: The roll should be slow and controlled with the legs pressed together and the ankles extended. Since the toes merely point to initiate the rolling action, the student does not land heavily on the head and neck area, which often happens because the student uses brute force to complete the skill instead of executing the skill through control of the center of gravity.

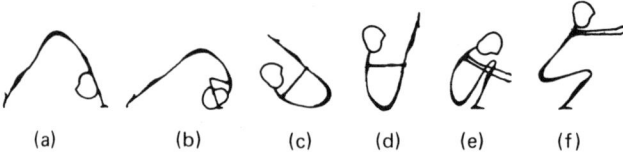

FORWARD ROLL TO SUPINE POSITION

Progression: Basic forward roll.

St. Pos.: Piked push-up position (a).

Sk. Init.: Lower the back of the head to the mat; point the toes to initiate lifting the hips over the head into the roll. As the roll continues down the spine, stretch the arms overhead on the mat and keep the head on the mat. The abdominals begin to relax lowering the legs slowly to the mat. (This roll works nicely into a floor exercise routine.)

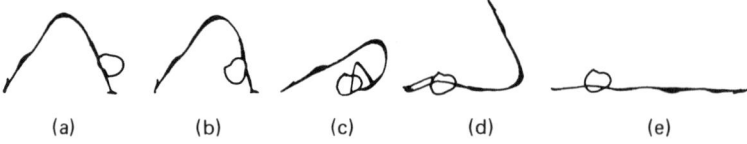

Variations:

1. From the supine position move the arms sideways at shoulder level. Lift the chest upward off the mat while the head maintains contact with the mat (b); press the arms off the mat and circle them over the head (c); move the arms forward toward the toes (d). The head follows and is lowered downward to the knees (e).

2. From the supine position (a) contract the abdominals. Lift the chest followed by the head while drawing the knees to the chest. The arms can either remain on the mat for support near the hips (d) or they can circle backward—upward over the head (e) to encircle the knees with the body in a tucked position (f).

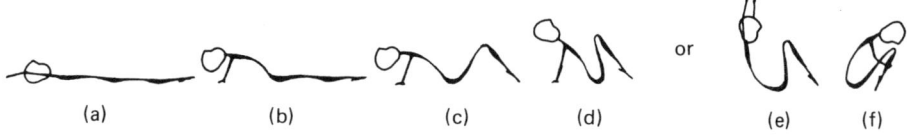

3. Contract the abdominals from the supine position. Lift the head, chest, and legs upward into a V position. The hands may remain on the mat near the hips or if the student is flexible, the hands may grasp the legs and pull them close to the chest and face.

4. From the supine position with arms stretched over the head roll sideways onto the stomach by lifting one hip upward and then forward over the other hip; the legs remain straight and together (b). [Student is now in a prone position and can execute

pose (c), then open legs to a straddle (d), push body back through a straddle sitting position (e) to any sitting pose (f).]

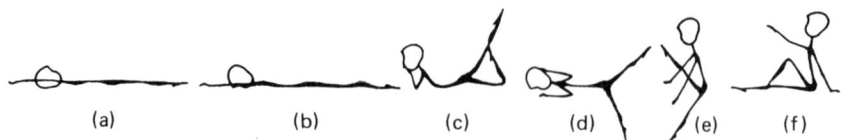

5. From the supine position lift one hip to initiate a roll onto the stomach and continue this rolling movement smoothly by lifting the shoulder to roll onto the back. During the roll from the prone position, sit up into a tuck or any sitting pose.

FORWARD ROLL TO KNEE SCALE

Progression: Assume the V-sit position with the hands on the mat near the hips. Rotate the right leg outward at the hip; bend the knee so that the lower leg crosses under the straight left leg. Rotate toward the right and execute either a one-quarter turn or a one-half turn as the body is raised upward into a kneeling position on the right knee. The left leg remains straight and does not touch the mat as it swings backward into the knee scale position. The hands contact the mat and the head lifts. Repeat the progression bending the left leg and turning to the left to assume the knee scale position.

From the V-sit position bend one leg. Place the lower leg under the straight leg. Then kneel upward and reach straight forward with the arms. Swing the straight leg sideways to the rear as the hands are placed on the mat in a knee scale position. (Since there is no turning action either to the left or the right, it does not matter which leg the student bends to get to this knee scale. It is important that the straight leg stays up off the mat as the student assumes the final position.)

St. Pos.: Pike push-up position (a).

Sk. Init.: Lower the head to the mat; point the toes (b) to initiate the rolling action down the spine (c). Roll into the V-sit position; then bend the desired leg as explained in progression (d). Turn toward this bent leg and raise upward into the knee scale position (e and f). To roll to a knee scale without turning, reach straight forward and upward while kneeling up on the flexed leg. Lower the hands to the mat as the straight leg circles sideways and backward to the knee scale position.

Forward Roll to Knee Scale With ½ Turn

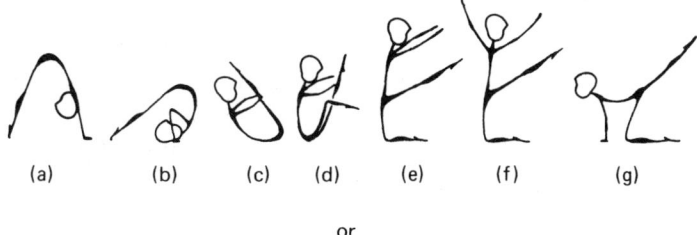

(a)　(b)　(c)　(d)　(e)　(f)　(g)

or

Forward Roll to Knee Scale Without Turning

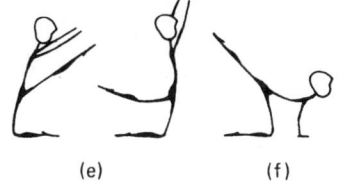

(e)　(f)

FORWARD ROLL TO HALF SPLIT

Progression: Forward roll to knee scales both with and without turns.

St. Pos.: Pike push-up position.

Sk. Init.: Lower into the roll as in a forward roll to the knee scale. Continue to the V-sit phase with one leg bent.

Recovery: To execute a one-quarter turn or a one-half turn into the half split, move out of the V-sit as follows: If the right leg is bent, lower that knee to the mat while turning to the right. The hands are not placed on the mat but are lifted overhead as the straight leg is lowered to the mat and the hips are raised to a resting position on the right heel. Reverse to turn to the left.

From this half split position the straight leg may be bent and the foot lifted toward the head to form a pose (f).

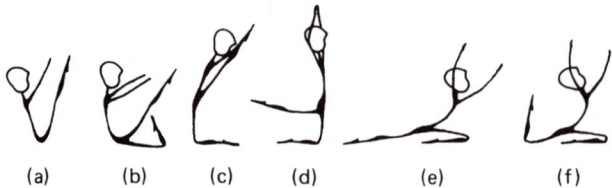

(a) (b) (c) (d) (e) (f)

This roll can be used going into the half split without any turning motion. Here the body raises upward onto the bent knee as the straight leg reaches forward and upward and is then rotated sideways and backward to be placed on the mat behind the hips. The hips are lowered to a sitting position on the heel of the bent leg.

FORWARD STRADDLE ROLL

Progression: From straddle sitting with the hands placed on the mat between the legs (a) lean forward and push downward with the shoulders. Attempt to get the hips to lift up off the mat (b). Some of the body weight must be maintained on the *feet* as well as on the hands. Repeat this pushing action but start in a straddled V-sit (1); reach for the mat between the legs and place the hands on the mat before the feet contact the floor (2). Then lean forward and push to clear the hips off the mat and to support the weight on the feet (3). If the students are strong, flexible, and have good timing, they can assume a straddled standing position from this progression.

(a) (b)   (1) (2) (3)

rolls

St. Pos.: From the pike push-up position or a straddled pike position (a).

Sk. Init.: Lower the back of the head to the mat as the toes point forcing the hips over the head and starting the rolling action (b). The legs remain straddled through the V-sit position (c) and the hands reach for the mat between the legs before the feet are lowered to the mat (d).

Recovery: As the hands contact the mat, press the shoulders downward, lean the upper body forward, and support the weight on the feet (e). Maintain the straddled pike standing position in preparation for the next roll (f).

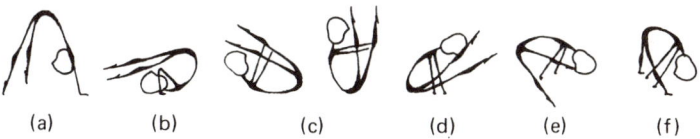

(a) (b) (c) (d) (e) (f)

Variations:

1. Roll to a straddle sit by lowering the legs to the mat from the V-sit position. Place one hand on the mat next to the hip; arch upward and toward that supporting arm as the free arm circles across the legs up over the supporting arm to an overhead position. Sit down and repeat the arch to the other side.

2. Roll to the above straddle sit. Then push the torso forward while closing the legs behind to a prone position. (The hands are placed on the mat close to the chest as the legs pass through the straddle to close behind, forming the prone position.)

FORWARD ROLL
ONE-QUARTER TURN TO SPLIT

Progression: Forward straddle roll.

St. Pos.: Pike push-up position.

Sk. Init.: Lower the back of the head to the mat. Point the toes to initiate the rolling action. Roll through the V-sit position and then open the legs into a straddle position.

Recovery: As the legs are lowered to the mat, turn toward the right to execute a stride split with the right leg forward. On the next roll turn to the left to assume a stride split with the left leg forward. The hands may be used close to the hips to assist in lifting the body to the split position at first. Once the skill is learned, attempt to keep the hands off the mat while moving into the split position.

Variations:

    1. From the split position work on leg flexibility by lowering the chest over the front leg and relaxing. After stretching in this position, sit up and arch backward with the arms overhead looking for the rear leg. If the back is flexible, grasp the rear leg with the hands.

    2. From the split position bend the back knee and lift the foot toward the head. The ankle of this leg is grasped by one hand and the leg is stretched by holding the foot close to the hips.

    3. From the V-sit position keep the legs straight and cross the right leg over the left. Rotate a one-quarter turn toward the left to assume a right split. Reverse for a left split.

FORWARD ROLL TO SPLIT

Progression: Assume a V-sit position on the mat with the hands on the mat near the hips. Rotate one leg outward from the hip and bend that leg so that the lower leg will cross under the extended leg. Lifting the torso, kneel upward onto the knee as the straight leg is extended forward and upward. Lower the straight leg to the mat and slide into the split position. The arms do not touch the mat. (To end in a split with the right leg forward, the left leg must bend during the V-sit phase.)

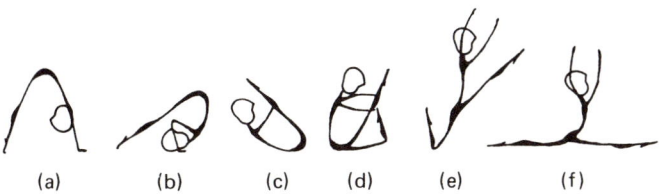

(a)   (b)   (c)   (d)   (e)   (f)

St. Pos.:   Piked push-up position (a).

Sk. Init.:   Lower the head to the mat and point the toes to initiate the rolling action (b). Reaching forward with the arms, roll to the V-sit position (c).

Recovery: From the V-sit position continue with the progression as explained above (d–f). To show leg amplitude, the forward split leg should be lifted high during the kneeling action and then lowered to the split. The arms should be used in a graceful pose.

**FORWARD ROLL
ONE-QUARTER TURN TO KNEELING POSITION**

Progression: Assume the V-sit position. Tuck both knees diagonally toward the left shoulder so that the feet are toward the right hip (d). Keeping the chest facing forward, begin to kneel up onto the knees as the hands and arms reach forward (e) and then upward overhead as the torso completes a one-quarter turn to the left (f); continue with another one-quarter turn (g) to the left with the torso and lower the hips to the other side of the knees (h); place the hands on the mat next to the hips and extend the legs into another V-sit position. Repeat this tuck to a kneeling turn to another V-sit several times.

St. Pos.:   Piked push-up position (a).

rolls

Sk. Init.: Lower the head to the mat and point the toes to initiate the rolling action (b). Roll through the V-sit position (c) with the arms reaching forward.

Recovery: While in the V-sit, tuck the knees (d) and continue with the turn as described in the progression above (e–h).

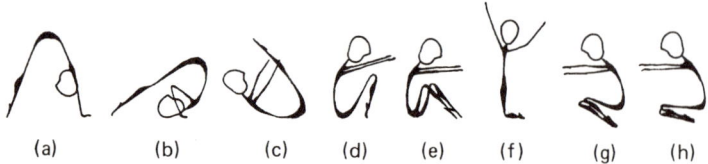

(a)　(b)　(c)　(d)　(e)　(f)　(g)　(h)

Variations:

1. From the above roll execute a backward roll to a kneeling position or any of the backward roll variations.

2. From the final tucked sitting position with the knees toward the right hip, the right hand on the mat near the right hip, and the left arm extended upward (i), kneel onto the right knee, arch the back and lift the hips toward the ceiling (j). From this arched position cross the left leg over the right thigh placing the foot near the right hand (k). Turn to the right on the left foot as the body extends to a standing position on the left leg (right leg extends upward) and then step onto the right leg. (l)

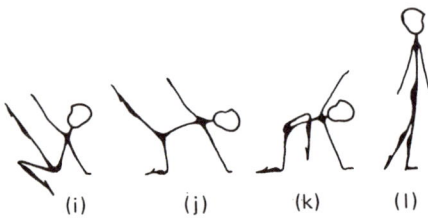

(i)　(j)　(k)　(l)

**FORWARD ROLL
TO KNEELING LUNGE POSITION**

Progression: Assume the V-sit position. Bend one knee and cross the lower leg under the straight leg (d). Lifting the chest forward and upward, kneel onto this knee as the straight leg reaches forward (e). Bend the forward leg and place the foot on the mat (f). Arch the hips forward and assume an arched kneeling lunge position (g). Repeat the progression, but bend the other leg to start the kneeling lunge.

St Pos.: Piked position push-up (a).

Sk. Init.: Lower the back of the head to the mat and initiate the roll by pointing the toes (b). Roll smoothly along the spine to V-sit (c).

Recovery: From the V-sit position reach forward with the arms as the body moves into the kneeling lunge (d–g) explained in the above progression. Once this lunge is assumed, the knee of the back leg may be flexed and the foot may be raised toward the head to form a final pose (h) with the arms held gracefully.

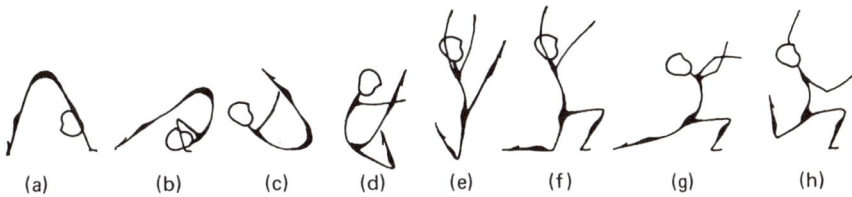

(a)   (b)   (c)   (d)   (e)   (f)   (g)   (h)

FORWARD ROLL TO LUNGE

Progression: Assume the V-sit position; rotate one leg outward at the hip; bend the knee so that it crosses under the straight leg (d). Kneel up onto this knee (e) and step forward onto the other leg (f). Keep the knee of the forward leg bent to support the body weight as the rear leg is extended into a standing lunge position (g).

St. Pos.: Piked push-up position or any other desired position (a).

Sk. Init.: Lower the back of the head to the mat (b). Point the toes to initiate the rolling action through the V-sit (c).

Recovery: From the V-sit position bend the desired leg (d) and continue with the progression as described above (e–g). Use the hands in a graceful pose.

Variation:

Roll to standing scale. From the kneeling position out of the V-sit step forward. Straighten this leg while lifting the rear leg backward and upward to a standing scale position (h).

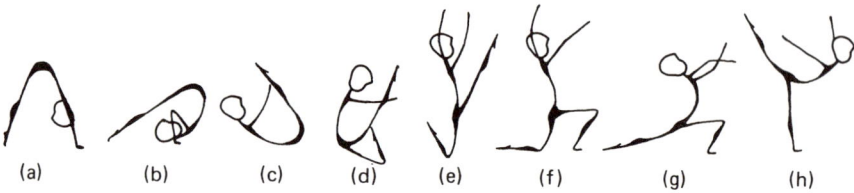

(a)　(b)　(c)　(d)　(e)　(f)　(g)　(h)

FORWARD ROLL TO JUMP

Progression: From a standing position practice jumping upward into the following positions, arch with legs together (a), stag (b), double stag (c), tuck (d), stradde, one-half turn, full turn, straddle toe touch (e). Go into the jump from a squat position with the arms reaching forward. The landing from this jump should be in an upright stand.

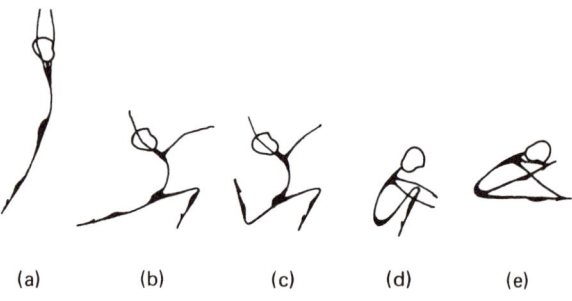

(a)　(b)　(c)　(d)　(e)

St. Pos.: Any forward roll position (a).

Sk. Init.: Lower the head to the mat. Point the toes to initiate the rolling action (b). Continue the controlled roll through a squat position with the arms reaching forward parallel to the floor (c–f).

Recovery: Immediately jump upward into one of the jump positions (g) and land in an erect stand ready to go into another roll. Do these rolls down the length of the tumbling mats. Execute a different jump after each roll and end the sequence with a one-half turning jump.

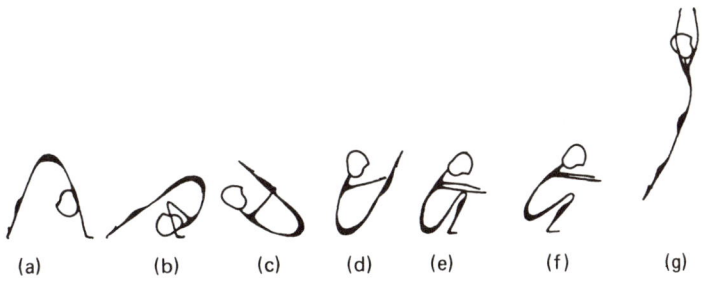

(a) (b) (c) (d) (e) (f) (g)

FORWARD ROLL TO A BODY WAVE

Progression: Practice body wave action from a standing position with the knees slightly relaxed and the arms reaching forward. (This wave action is explained from a squat position.) Assume a squat position with one foot slightly ahead of the other, arms reaching forward, and palms upward. Slowly lower the arms downward as the hips press forward and the knees begin to extend to an erect standing position. Continue to circle the arms backward and upward to a stretched overhead position which should be reached as the body completely extends. Arch the head and chest backward as the hips begin to press forward. Then press the chest forward. By the time the body is extended the head is in a stretched upright position.

St. Pos.: Piked push-up position or any other desired position.

Sk. Init.: Lower the head to the mat and point the toes to initiate the rolling action.

Recovery: From the V-sit position bend the knees and place the feet on the mat with one slightly ahead of the other; arms reach forward with the palms upward. As the body assumes this squat position, the body waving action begins. The body wave movement gives the beginner an awkward feeling. Once perfected it is a beautifully supple movement, and can be performed from numerous starting positions.

FORWARD ROLL WITHOUT HANDS

Progression: From a lunge position place the hands on the mat so that the arms are spread wide apart. Try to maintain the body weight on the forward lunging leg rather than on the hands. Lower the back of the head to the mat as the hands push slightly. To begin the rolling action, lift the back leg upward and over the head. The forward leg merely extends and the toes point. Join the legs together before the V-sit position is reached. From the V-sit recover to a lunge position as explained on page 18. Repeat this progression from the new lunge position.

St. Pos.: Forward stride lunge position, back arched, head back with arms overhead in a graceful pose.

Sk. Init.: Keep the arms straight and move them sideways at shoulder level. Lean the torso forward. Reach forward of the supporting leg and place the *back* of the hands on the mat; the arms remain straight. Tuck the chin to the chest and lower the back of the head to the mat. Initiate the rolling action by lifting the rear leg upward and forward over the head; press with the backs of the hands and roll to the V-sit position.

Recovery: From the V-sit position bend a knee and kneel upward into another lunge in order to prepare to repeat the no-handed forward rolls down the mat.

FORWARD STRADDLE ROLL WITHOUT HANDS

This skill takes flexibility and timing.

St. Pos.: Straddle stand; body piked forward with hands grasping ankles (a).

Sk. Init.: Reach forward with the head and chest in order to force a loss of balance in the forward direction (b). As the balance is lost, tuck the chin to the chest and place the back of the head on the mat (c). The toes point pressing the hips over the head into the rolling action.

Recovery: Remain in the straddled pike position and maintain the grasp on the ankles (d). As the feet contact the mat (e), push on the ankles while lifting the hips forward and upward into the straddled starting position (f and g). Since the hands do not release the ankles, you are in the starting position to continue another no-handed straddle roll. (Since this skill is difficult, proper timing of standing onto the feet while pushing downward on the ankles and reaching forward and upward with the hips is necessary to be successful.)

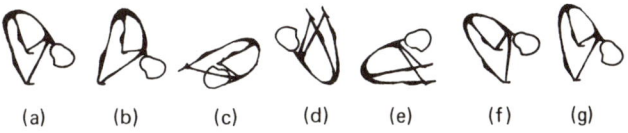

(a)　(b)　(c)　(d)　(e)　(f)　(g)

FORWARD ROLL INTO HANDSTAND BALANCE

Progression: Handstand (page 62); handstand into forward roll (page 66); Arabian limber (page 82).

St. Pos.: Piked push-up position (a).

Sk. Init.: Lower the back of the head to the mat and point the toes to initiate the rolling action (b). Complete the roll to a squatting position with arms reaching forward (c–e).

Recovery: From the squat position at the completion of the roll (e) continue reaching the arms forward as the hands are placed on the mat in front of the body (f), lift the hips upward toward the shoulders (g); keep the arms straight as the legs extend until the feet thrust off the mat. Now move the hips directly above the shoulders, tuck the legs so that the heels touch the hips (h), and continue to press the shoulders downward as the legs are extended upward into the handstand position (i). (The arms do not bend during this jump into the handstand position. The student can execute another roll from the handstand and immediately jump upward to another handstand continuing the rolling action along the length of the mat.)

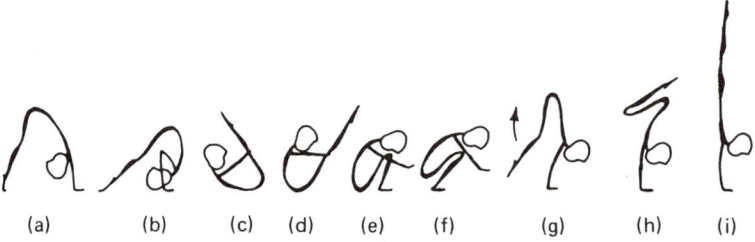

(a)   (b)   (c)   (d)   (e)   (f)   (g)   (h)   (i)

Variations:

    1. From the squat position extend the legs into the handstand position by passing through a straddle. [This action takes place after (g).]

    2. From (g) keep the legs straight and together and kick into the handstand through a pike position. This takes a great deal of lift followed by an upward driving action by the heels.

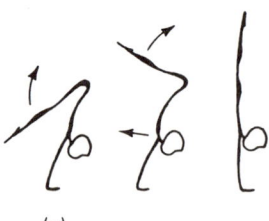

(g)

Students can work on each of these variations continuously down the length of the mat. As each variation is mastered, they can alternate the body positions used before extending into the handstand position.

DIVING FORWARD ROLL

Progression: From a standing position jump off both feet into a handstand position. (Students should start this progression by having the hands close to the mat so that they merely have to place them down as they jump forward.) As students learn to support the body weight on the arms from a small jump, they should be encouraged to extend their starting position. The emphasis should be placed on the height of the jump into the handstand position (jump up, reaching upward, lifting the hips upward; as the body pikes downward, heels lift backward and upward and the hands reach for the mat). The horizontal distance covered by the roll should not be stressed. This is not a skill for the beginning tumbler. Students should work on the progression jump into the handstand position and learn to control the handstand into the forward roll before executing the diving roll. Once these progressions have been learned, the tumbler combines the jump into the handstand with the handstand into the forward roll so that there is a continuous movement.

The skill should be practiced continuously down the length of the mat. The student jumps through the handstand position and immediately lowers into the roll; as the body passes into the squat position, the arms reach upward and the student should immediately jump upward into the next diving roll.

FORWARD ROLL TO KNEE SPIN

Progression: Assume a V-sit position on the mat; rotate the right leg outward at the hip; bend the knee and cross the right lower leg under the extended left leg. Kneel up onto the right knee (keeping the left leg extended forward) and begin to spin to the right; bend the left knee and step into a spin on that knee; lift the right leg while spinning on the left knee and stand up into an extended position on the right leg while reaching upward with the arms. The left leg is extended backward. Walk slowly through this knee spinning action several times. Then add more momentum so that the body spins at least one-half turn on each knee.

St. Pos.: Pike push-up position or any other desired forward roll position.

Sk. Init.: Lower the back of the head to the mat and initiate the rolling action by pointing the toes. Reaching forward with the arms, roll through the V-sit position.

Recovery: From this V-sit position continue into the spin by bending the right leg and continuing with the progression as explained above.

Variation:

If students can do splits, they can work on the forward roll to knee spin into a split. To land in a split with the right leg forward, spin to the right on the right knee; then continue to spin on the left knee while extending the right leg forward and upward; as the spin is completed on the left knee, arch the back and fall forward into the split position.

KICK-BACK FORWARD ROLL

Progression: Execute the skill as described below by moving slowly and bending the supporting leg in order to place the hands on the mat. Push with the hands and gently lower the head to the mat to complete the roll as described on next page.

St. Pos.: Standing erect, arms by sides.

Sk. Init.: While standing erect, lift the left leg forward and upward; then swing it down and back upward as the chest is lowered forward so that the hands can be placed on the mat. Keep the supporting right leg straight as you lose your balance into the roll. Continue to lift the left leg as the right ankle extends pressing off the mat. Join the legs together at this point.

Recovery: From the V-sit position with the legs together bend the left leg and cross the lower leg under the extended right leg; kneel up onto the left knee; then stand upon the right leg. Lift the left leg forward and then drive it downward and backward into another kick-back forward roll.

Variation:

No-Handed Kick-Back Forward Roll: Practice the basic no-handed forward roll (page 22). The starting position and the skill initiation is as explained above; however, as the leg kicks back upward, the chest is lowered with the arms stretched sideways at shoulder level. The back of the head is placed on the mat; arms do not touch the mat. The recovery is the same as in above skill.

BACKWARD ROLL PROGRESSIONS

1. Sit in the tuck position with the hands near the shoulders and with palms up and the fingers pointing backward (a). Roll backward to the shoulders so that *while* the chin is on the chest the head is on the mat (b); place the hands under the shoulders with the fingers pointing toward the hips and with the elbows pointing toward the ceiling. Extend the legs over the head placing the toes down toward the mat. Stay in this position to stretch the back muscles while attempting to touch the toes to the mat (c). After several seconds shove off the mat with the hands and return rolling along the spine to the starting position (a). Repeat this progression several times to program the students to roll back with the chin tucked to the chest and then place the toes *down* onto the mat. (While learning the backward roll beginners tend

to extend the legs upward to the ceiling as they lift upward with the head. This causes the neck to support the body weight and the muscles become stiff and sore. The above progression should give the student the kinesthetic awareness of a safe beginning for the backward roll without taking the chance of having the neck muscles support the total body weight.)

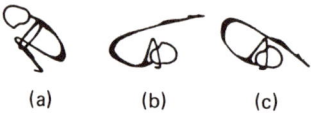

(a)   (b)   (c)

2. Repeat the above progression placing the weight on the toes after they touch the mat (d) (the knees will have to bend slightly to accomplish this). Return to the starting position by pushing with the hands. This progression should be practiced several times so that you can now roll back and immediately place the toes downward onto the mat supporting some of the body weight on the toes.

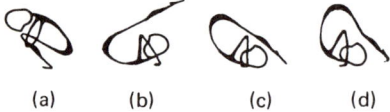

(a)   (b)   (c)   (d)

3. Practice the pike position push-ups with the chin tucked to the chest touching the back of the head to the mat. (This exercise was explained on page 8). Encourage students to press off the mat with the head as well as with the hands while the hips move from an over-the-head position to the new base position above the feet. If necessary, the students can bend the knees to return to the new base.

By noticing the movement of the hips the teacher can immediately find the students who attempt to do all the work with their arm and shoulder muscles rather than by merely shifting their center of gravity to a position over the new base.

BACKWARD ROLL

St. Pos.: Squat on the mat with the body tucked, the chin on the chest, and the hands near the shoulders (a).

Sk. Init: Combine progressions 2 and 3 on page 30. Roll backward to the top of the shoulders so that the head touches the mat while the chin is still on the chest (b); place the feet downward onto the mat and put weight on the toes (c) as the arms and head push off the mat (d). Move the hips backward and upward from an over-the-head position toward the new base, the feet (e). The knees should not touch the mat. Press hard with the arms so that elbows extend during the roll. If the tuck position is maintained, the vertebrae will roll smoothly down the mat.

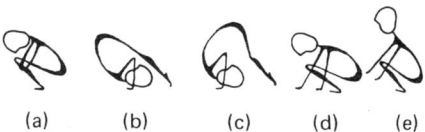

(a) (b) (c) (d) (e)

Spotting: Stand to the student's side during the roll. Be ready to move in to grasp the hips as the student gets into the piked position with the hands placed correctly (elbows pointing to the ceiling) and the toes down on the mat. Face the student's back. Bend your knees and place your hands on the student's hips. Tell the student to push and stand as you straighten your legs in order to lift the student over his head and onto his feet. This action allows the spotter to lift with the leg muscles rather than the weaker back muscles. Do not rush in to spot before checking the correct pike position. This precaution eliminates some of the spotter's work.

BACKWARD ROLL TO KNEE SCALE

St. Pos.:

1. Squat with the body tucked, the chin on the chest, and the hands by the shoulders (a).

2. Stand with the hands by the sides (the student will bend the knees to lower into the roll or pike forward to lower into the roll).

3. Stand in the forward stride position with the weight supported on the rear leg. The rear leg bends to lower the hips to the mat for the roll.

4. Stand on one leg with the other leg lifted and with the arms forward or overhead. The supporting leg bends to lower the hips to the mat for the roll.

Sk. Init.: Lower the hips to the mat and roll backward while keeping the chin tucked to the chest (b). As the legs extend over the head (c), lower one leg downward toward the mat and extend the other leg backward and upward at a 45 degree angle with the horizontal (d).

Recovery: Place the weight on the toes touching the mat, push with the arms, and lift the head (e). The extended leg continues to stretch backward and upward as the base leg bends lowering the knee gently to the mat. Assume the knee scale position (f).

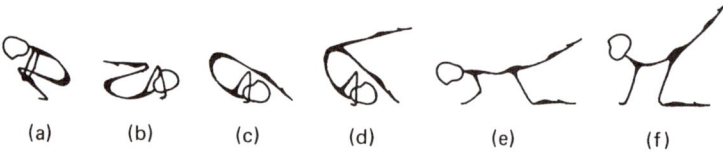

(a)   (b)   (c)   (d)   (e)   (f)

Variations:

1. Upon landing in the knee scale position, bend the extended leg and touch the foot to the head (g).

(g)

2. From the piked position (d) with one leg on the mat, roll over the head lowering body into half split position with the

chest held high (h) or with the chest lower over the forward knee (i).

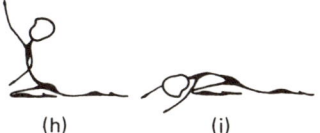

3. Upon reaching the half split position (h), bend the extended leg and touch the foot to the head.

BACKWARD ROLL TO BOTH KNEES

St. Pos.: Same as in the backward roll to knee scale (a).

Sk. Init.: Roll backward (b) while lowering both legs to the mat with the ankles extended (c) so that the top of the toes and insteps contact the mat (d).

Recovery: Press the weight onto the toes, push with the hands, and lift the head (e) as the hips are lifted over the head and the knees are gently lowered to the mat. Assume a tucked kneeling position (f).

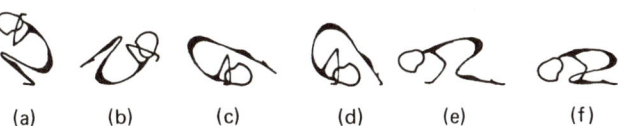

Variations:

1. Recover to a kneeling position with the hips on the heels, the torso extended, and the arms overhead.

2. Recover to a stretched kneeling position.

BACKWARD ROLL TO PRONE POSITION

St. Pos.: Any of the positions listed for the backward roll to knee scale (a).

Sk. Init.: Maintaining a tight tuck position (b), roll backward. Keeping the legs extended, lower both pointed toes.

Recovery: As the toes contact the mat, place the weight on the toes (d) and insteps as the hips are lifted overhead (e). As the hips pass overhead, push so that the toes slide along the mat to a stretched prone position (f). (The arms must push hard as the head lifts to complete a smooth movement. If the arms continue to press away from the mat and there is little friction the student will end in a prone position with the arms extended above the head.) Assume a pose by arching the back (g) and lifting the feet to the head (h).

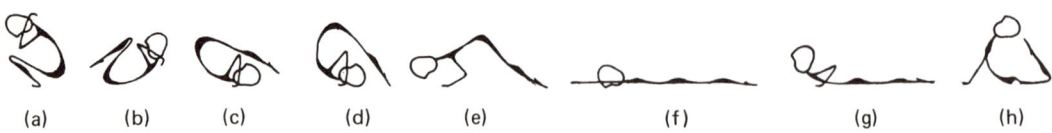

(a)　(b)　(c)　(d)　(e)　(f)　(g)　(h)

BACKWARD ROLL TO LUNGE

St. Pos.: Standing or in any desired position as described in the backward, roll to the knee scale.

Sk. Init.: Lower the hips to the mat and roll the body backward keeping the chin tucked to the chest (b). Extend the legs backward and upward at a 45°-angle with the horizontal (c).

Recovery: As the legs extend backward and upward in a thrusting manner, push the arms, lift the head, and step one leg in close to the hands while the other leg remains straight continuing the extension backward and upward (d). As weight is placed on the forward leg, lift the torso. This action lowers the rear leg into a lunge position (e).

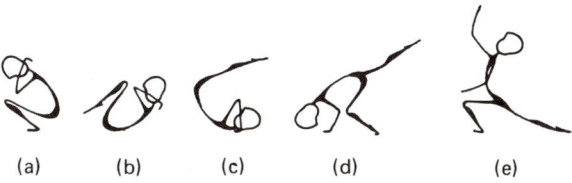

(a)   (b)   (c)   (d)   (e)

BACKWARD STRADDLE ROLL

St. Pos.: Assume the straddle standing position with the upper body piked forward reaching between the legs with the arms, hands close together, and palms facing the mat. Keep the arms close to the body. Do not place the hands on the mat from this position.

Sk. Init.: Keeping the arms close to the thigh area, sit backward and reach for the mat with the hands and briefly support the body weight on the hands so that the hips can be gently lowered to the mat. Keep the body in the pike position with the back rounded so that the chin is on the chest as the roll is continued along the spine. The legs, while straddled, are lifted overhead and the feet are placed down on the mat. As the weight is transferred from the hands to the hips, quickly move the hands to the shoulder position for the completion of the backward roll.

Recovery: Keeping the legs straddled and straight, lower the feet to the mat and place the weight on the feet as the hips are lifted up over the feet. Lift the head as the shoulders push away from the mat. This action makes you assume the straddled starting position. If the hips are used correctly, very little arm extension is necessary to roll over the head and to come to the straddled standing position.

Variations:
  1. Lower into straddle split after the straddle roll.
  2. Begin lowering into the straddle split and keeping the feet in place execute a one-quarter turn with the hips continuing to lower into a stride split. (Turn to the right to land in a split with the right leg forward; turn to the left for a left split.)
  3. From the recovery to the straddle stand continue to sit backward. Lower the chest to touch the floor with the arms stretched at shoulder level.

Spotting: As the student begins the roll, you should stand at the student's side so that you can slow the downward fall onto the hands by placing one hand on the student's back and the other hand under the thigh close to the hips. Keep the student in a pike position and with a lifting action on the thigh slowly lower the hips to the mat. As the student rolls to the top of the shoulders and head, step in and face the student's back. Check to see that the basic roll position is correct (hands under shoulders, feet down on the mat, legs straddled and straight, feet placed on the mat close to the shoulder area), grasp the hips, and tell the student to push and stand as you lift the hips up over the head and then over the feet.

BACKWARD PIKE ROLL

Progression: Backward straddle roll.

St. Pos.: Assume a piked standing position with the legs straight and together. Hold the arms at either sides of the legs at the thigh area (a).

Sk. Init.: Lower the chest toward the knees. Extend the hips backward while reaching for the mat with the hands (b). The weight is momentarily supported by the arms as the hips are gently lowered to the mat. As the weight is transferred from the hands to the hips, move the hands quickly to the shoulder area in order to complete the roll (c).

Recovery: The body continues the rolling action while maintaining the piked position as the feet are placed on the mat (d). Push the arms and lift the head as the hips are raised backward and upward (e) to the piked standing starting position (f).

Spotting: Similar to the spotting for the backward straddle roll.

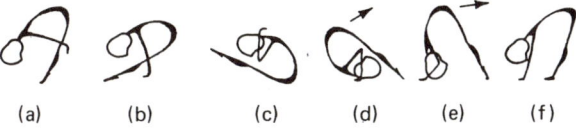

(a)　(b)　(c)　(d)　(e)　(f)

BACKWARD ROLL TO HEADSTAND

Progression: Headstand balance and variations to the headstand balance. Backward roll variations.

St. Pos.: Any of the backward roll starting positions. The beginning student may wish to use the squat position (a).

St. Pos.: Staying in the tight tuck position (b), roll backward onto the shoulders. Look at the toes and thrust the legs upward toward the ceiling (c). During the thrust phase extend the arms and lift the head slightly to settle in a comfortable headstand position (d). Quickly reposition the hands to block the momentum of the roll (d and e).

Recovery:
1. From the headstand straddle the legs, tuck the hips, lower the feet to the mat in line with the hands, and push the hips backward going into a backward straddle roll.
2. Lower through a straddle, then rotate into a stride split.
3. Lower one leg to the mat, bend the knee, then push up into a knee scale position.
4. Pike down and touch the toes to the mat; then assume a kneeling position on both knees.
5. Execute a forward roll from the headstand by piking at the hips. Tuck the chin to the chest as the arms push causing the hips to pass overhead into the roll.
6. During the headstand tuck the knees downward toward the chest; then thrust the legs upward toward the ceiling as the arms extend to lift the body into a handstand position.

See the headstand balance (page 55) for a variety of pose positions to assume while in this balance.

Spotting: Stand to the side of the student and be ready to grasp the near ankle as soon as the student reaches position (c). Keeping the head well back, time your lifting efforts with the student's leg thrust and balance the headstand position while reminding the student to change the hand position quickly. (Little lift is needed and this should be accomplished by merely extending the legs rather than lifting up with only the arms and back.)

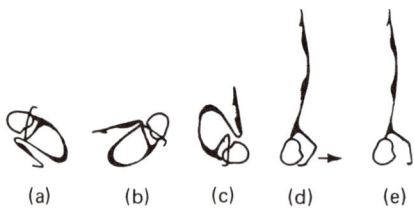

(a) (b) (c) (d) (e)

BACKWARD ROLL TO FOREARM STAND

Progression: Backward roll to a headstand (page 35); forearm balance and variations (page 60).

St. Pos.: Squat with the hands near the shoulder area (a).

Sk. Init.: Execute a roll similar to the backward roll to the headstand position. As you roll to the top of the head (d), do not move the hands to block the momentum; instead, lower the elbows to the mat as the head is lifted and the back arches (e). The force of the roll is absorbed by the elbows and the arching action of the back (f).

Recovery:
    1. Lower one leg at a time to a knee scale position.
    2. Lower one leg at a time to the kneeling half split position.
    3. Pike the hips and tuck the chin to the chest to initiate a forward roll out of the forearm balance.
    4. Arch the back. Lower the feet to the mat in a back bend position as the arms press and extend off the mat so that a limber action from the forearm balance is completed.

Spotting: Similar to the backward roll to the headstand balance. After the slight lift needed to clear the head, allow for the necessary back arch.

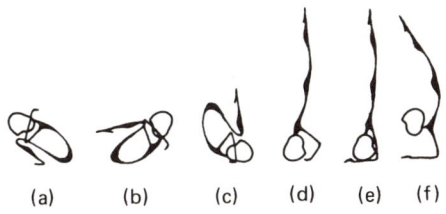

(a)   (b)   (c)   (d)   (e)   (f)

BACKWARD ROLL TO HANDSTAND (BACK EXTENDED ROLL)

St. Pos.: Stand or squat (a).

Sk. Init.: Roll backward onto shoulders (b) and extend the legs to a low pike position (c). Watch the knees and thrust the legs straight upward toward the ceiling as the arms extend and the head lifts. The leg thrust and the arm and head extension must be timed exactly in order to reach the handstand position with a minimum of effort (d).

Recovery: From the handstand position press hard with the shoulders and lower one leg in a controlled manner to the mat. As the foot contacts the mat and the weight is placed on the leg, lift the torso. This lifting action lowers the extended leg.

Spotting: Stand at the student's side and prepare to grasp the near leg during the leg thrust phase of the skill. Lift the student into a balanced handstand position.

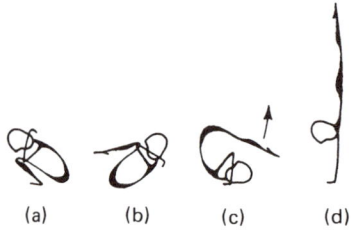

(a)　　(b)　　(c)　　(d)

Variations:

1. From the handstand position press with the shoulders and pike the legs downward in a slow controlled manner.
2. From the handstand straddle the legs and press with the shoulders as the legs are lowered to a straddle stand or a straddle or stride split.
3. From the handstand press with the shoulders and pike the legs downward in a slow controlled manner while bending the knees and lowering to a kneeling position.
4. Same as (2), but straddle through to a balanced straddle and hold with the body weight supported on the hands.
5. Pike at the hips, tuck the chin to the chest, and lower the shoulders gently to the mat by bending the elbows to initiate a forward roll.
6. Arch over into a front limber or forward walkover (pages 79 and 83).

rolls

7. From the handstand one arm pushes off to initiate a one-half turn to another handstand balance; the body is then lowered into a forward roll.

8. From the stretched handstand position lower to a forearm balance by bending either both arms at once or one arm at a time.

9. Fish-Flop: From the handstand position immediately lift the head upward as the elbows bend. Lower the chest to the mat and roll down to a prone position.

BACKWARD ROLL TO A WIDE ARM HANDSTAND

Progression: Backward roll to a handstand (page 37).

St. Pos.: Squatting position or standing position (a).

Sk. Init.: Roll backward (b) onto the shoulders in a low pike position but do not place the hands on the mat next to the shoulders; instead, straighten the arms and place the palms on the mat with the arms extended at shoulder level but slightly toward the head (c).

Recovery: The leg thrust and the head lift are similar to the thrusting action used in the backward roll to the handstand. The arms remain straight and press against the mat during the leg thrust phase thus raising the body into a wide arm handstand balance (d). The beginner will try this skill by practicing a backward roll to a handstand and progressively moving the hands to a wider position with each attempt.

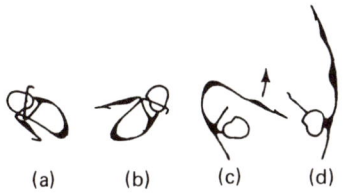

(a)   (b)   (c)   (d)

BACKWARD ROLL WITHOUT HANDS

This skill takes control of the center of gravity and increases neck strength.

Progression: Beginning students should practice back straddle rolls with the use of the hands but lessen the arm pushing action with each attempt. If they can roll over the head in a comfortable manner without supporting the body weight on the hands, they should continue with the following skill.

St. Pos.: Piked straddle stand with hands grasping the ankles (a).

Sk. Init.: Sit backward (b) to initiate the roll (c). Keep the spine flexed so that the back rolls smoothly along the mat (d). Keep legs straight and straddled; continue to grasp the ankles with the hands.

Recovery: Place the feet on the mat and attempt to keep them as much as possible in line with the head (e). Place weight on feet as the head lifts; this forces the hips back up over the feet (f).

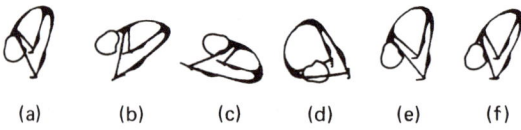

(a) (b) (c) (d) (e) (f)

BACKWARD ROLL TO CHEST STAND

Progression: Chest stand (page 60, variation 6).

St. Pos.: Stand or squat (a).

Sk. Init.: (Similar to the backward roll to a wide arm handstand, page 39) Roll backward to the pike position on the shoulders. Place the left arm on the mat in an extended position toward the left hip; the right arm is slightly bent placing the hand on the mat slightly above the right shoulder (c). The arms press as the legs thrust gently upward while the body executes a one-quarter turn rolling over the left shoulder into the chest stand position (d).

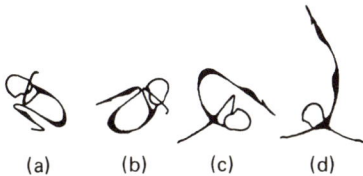

(a)   (b)   (c)   (d)

Variation:

From the balanced chest stand assume any pose found on page 61, variation (6).

TUCK POSITION SIDE ROLL

St. Pos.: Kneeling position with the hips on the heels and the torso tucked to the knees.

Sk. Init.: Maintaining the tuck position with the knees pulled tightly to the chest, lean to the right and roll over the back. Then continue rolling until the body is once again in the starting position. Repeat the roll toward the left. Notice that the knees *do not* leave the tuck position during the roll.

Variations:

1. Upon completion of the roll, extend the torso upward into a kneeling pose. Then curl downward again to roll in the opposite direction.

2. Execute the side roll to a sitting pose or a half split position.

3. From the starting position roll to the right; when on the back extend the right leg upward toward the ceiling; the left leg remains tucked to the chest. As the left knee touches the mat, kneel upward and place the extended right leg on the mat in a sideways lunge position. From this position tuck the chest to the knee and roll to the left while extending the left leg and bending the right as the body rolls over the back. Finish in the kneeling lunge position on the right knee.

4. Roll as in (3); as the left knee contacts the mat, turn to the right while placing the right foot on the mat and stand up on this leg. Continue turning to the right.

FORWARD SHOULDER ROLL

St. Pos.: Lunge position with the right leg forward (a).

Sk. Init.: Pike forward twisting the shoulders to the right and drawing the left shoulder toward the right ankle (b). Extend the left arm and place the right hand on the mat to lower gently into the roll. Roll over the left shoulder, diagonally across the back (c), and regain a balanced position by kneeling on the left knee and then stepping forward onto the right leg (d).

Variations:

1. Roll across the shoulder and back into a sitting posed position.

2. Execute a roll and while on the back (c) place the legs together. Tuck the knees to the chest and kneel up onto both knees.

3. Start the shoulder roll from a kneeling position and finish as in variation (1) or (2) or in the basic shoulder roll.

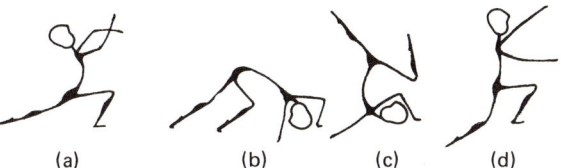

(a)　　　(b)　　(c)　　(d)

BACKWARD SHOULDER ROLL

St. Pos.: Squatting position or from a supine position.

Sk. Init.: Roll onto the shoulders while drawing the legs into a piked position toward the left shoulder. Extend the left arm toward the left hip and place the right hand next to the right shoulder with the elbow pointing toward the ceiling.

Recovery: Lower both toes to the mat with the ankles extended so that the body weight is supported on the insteps. Head looks to left but is held above the right shoulder as the hands push to move the hips over the left shoulder. Finish in a tucked kneeling position.

Variations:
1. Finish in a knee scale position.
2. Finish in a sitting pose position.
3. Finish in a half split position.

ADDITIONAL FORWARD ROLL VARIATIONS

ADDITIONAL FORWARD ROLL VARIATIONS

ADDITIONAL FORWARD ROLL VARIATIONS

ADDITIONAL BACKWARD ROLL VARIATIONS

ADDITIONAL BACKWARD ROLL VARIATIONS

ADDITIONAL SIDE/SHOULDER ROLL VARIATIONS

ADDITIONAL SIDE/SHOULDER ROLL VARIATIONS

2

inverted balances

TRI-POD BALANCE

St. Pos.: Place the hands and head on the mat to form a triangle. Fingers point straight ahead. (Student is on the feet, not the knees, with the hips held high.) A 90°-angle should be formed at the elbows and shoulders. Elbows should be positioned directly above the hands.

Sk. Init.: With head and hands in the above position, place the inside of the right knee to the outside of the right elbow and kneel heavily on the elbow (the left foot is still in contact with the mat). Once weight is placed on the elbow, place the left knee on the outside of the left elbow, kneel heavily on this elbow, and then extend the ankle by lifting the left toes from the mat. Maintain balance by dividing the weight between the head and the hands. Students must be encouraged to push hard with the hands while kneeling heavily on the elbows.

Spotting: Kneel to the right side of the student. As the right knee is placed on the right elbow, support that ankle by placing your left hand on the shin side of the ankle. (If students need your assistance, they will press that ankle downward into your hand. If help isn't needed, you are merely in a ready position.) Your right hand is placed on the mid-back area of the student's spine. Keep the student in balance as the left knee is placed on the left elbow. Give verbal cues to push with the hands in order to share in supporting the body weight with the head. Notice the placement of the hips. If they are directly over the head, the student is supporting the total body weight on the neck which is uncomfortable.

Variations:

    1. Control Tri-Pod: Practice controlling the center of gravity by shifting the hips from over the head toward the hands so that the hands are supporting most of the weight; shift the hips toward the head so that the head is supporting most of the weight; shift the hips again to center the center of gravity between the hands and head.

    2. Tri-Pod Forward Roll: From the balanced position (a) shift weight toward the hands. Press hard with the arms (b), tuck the chin to the chest so that the back of the head contacts the mat (c), move the hips beyond the head, and go into the forward roll (d) ending in a standing position or any of the forward roll variations listed in Chapter 1.

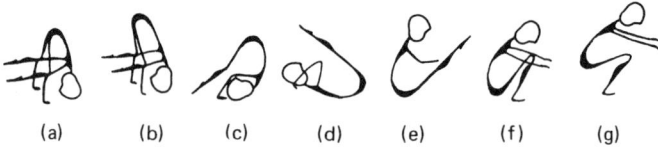

(a)   (b)   (c)   (d)   (e)   (f)   (g)

Spotting: From the spotting position explained for the basic tri-pod, grasp the student's right thigh with your left hand and move the hips toward the arms. Assist in tucking the chin to the chest by placing the right hand on the back of the student's head;

inverted balances

then lead the hips into the roll with the left hand. Keep the right hand on the back of the student's head during the roll. This makes it possible for the spotter to push the student into a standing position at the completion of the roll.

TIP-UP BALANCE

St. Pos.: From the tri-pod position explained previously, shift the hips toward the hands. *Kneel heavily* on the elbows (b). *Press* with the *fingertips* and *slowly* lift the head while continuing to push downward with the arms. Maintain balance for several seconds and then assume a squatting position.

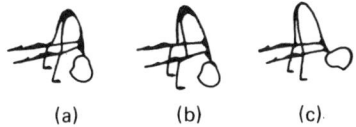

(a)   (b)   (c)

Spotting: Use the instructions for tri-pod spotting for the starting position. Then, if necessary, grasp the student's thigh and shift the hips toward the hands while giving verbal cues to push with the hands and fingers as the head is lifted.

Variations:
    1. Control Tip-Up: Move from the tri-pod balance into the tip-up balance. Then gently return to the tri-pod balance.
    2. From the tri-pod balance move to the tip-up balance. Then tuck the chin to the chest to go into a forward roll. Finish either standing or with any of the forward roll variations listed in Chapter 1.

EXTENDED TRI-POD BALANCE

Beginners often have difficulty learning a headstand because they cannot feel how to lift their hips upward over their heads. Beginners tend to maintain a low center of gravity while kicking the feet upward toward the ceiling. This action doesn't get them into a balanced position and it is hard on the neck muscles. In order to teach the class the feeling of lifting the hips, the extended tri-pod should be presented before having the students work on the headstand balance. This progression takes control of the center of gravity and once this control is mastered it is easier to learn the headstand balance.

St. Pos.: From the tri-pod position (a) lift the hips upward over the head, tuck the legs, and lift the heels to the hips. Thighs should now be parallel to the mat (b). Return slowly to the balanced tri-pod position (a).

Spotting: Observe students while they are practicing. Make sure that the heels are only lifted to the hips, not beyond. Watch the student's center of gravity and guide the hips into the correct position manually. At the same time give verbal cues. Students often need to be reminded to keep some of the body weight supported on their hands. If a manual assist is necessary, stand to the student's side and help lift the hips upward. Tell the student to push with the hands. Keep your face back from the kicking area and place your knee close to the student's back so that you can stop the student from overbalancing and falling.

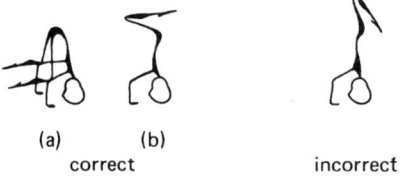

(a)   (b)
correct   incorrect

Variations:

1. Start from the tri-pod; hold balance for 3 seconds. Go into the extended tri-pod; hold 3 seconds. Return to the tri-pod; hold 3 seconds. Balance in the tip-up; hold 3 seconds. Return to the standing position on the feet. This exercise will help students gain the kinesthetic awareness needed for controlled work.

2. Tri-pod to extended tri-pod; hold. Tuck down almost to the tri-pod position and then go into a forward roll.

inverted balances

3. Tri-pod to extended tri-pod; straddle legs; tuck hips under so that the feet can be placed on the mat in line with the hands while the legs remain straddled; move the hips back as the arms push off the mat; replace the hands on the mat between the legs but closer to the hips and push to sit back gently onto the hips. After practicing this variation follow it with a back straddle roll ending in another backward roll variation from Chapter 1.

HEADSTAND BALANCE

Progressions: Tri-pod balance; extended tri-pod balance.

St. Pos.: Basic tri-pod position.

Sk. Init.: Lift the hips and legs to a momentary extended tri-pod balance with the thighs parallel to mat and the heels to the hips. *Slowly* extend the legs by reaching the toes to the ceiling. The body position while in the headstand should be *slightly inclined* toward the hands so that the center of gravity is centered within the base, not close to the forward edge of the base.

To practice controlling the center of gravity, move the legs through various positions while in the headstand balance. See the pose positions below:

Stag   Double Stag   Split   Bent Leg Split   Straddle

Variations:

1. Combine pose combinations by moving from the basic balance to a stag; return to the starting position; then move to a stag pose with the other leg forward; straighten the forward leg and open to a split pose; switch to the opposite split position; bend both knees to form the double stag pose; straighten the legs to split; then rotate the legs around to the straddle position. From

inverted balances

this position execute either variation (3) of the extended tri-pod or the following variation (2).

2. **Rotating Headstand:** (Rotate about the vertical axis while in the headstand.) This is easiest from the straddle position. Move each hand one at a time to the right side; then quickly twist the head to the right. Repeat this hand, hand, head rhythm until the rotation has been completed. After learning this turning action, practice the turn with the legs held together and straight in the basic headstand position or in any of the pose positions.

3. **Headstand, Straddle-Down:** (Use the tri-pod and extended tri-pod variation (3), page 55, as a progression.) Assume the balanced headstand position with the body slightly inclined toward the hands; open the legs to the straddle position; then rotate the hips under; place the feet in line with the hands; sit back gently and go into a backward straddle roll (see page 33).

Spotting: When the student is in the balanced headstand position, move to face the student's back. Hold the hips as the student straddles the legs. Help to rotate the hips under if necessary. As the feet are placed on the mat in line with the hands, help to lift the hips up and backward. As the student pushes with the arms and begins to sit back, slide your hands to the shoulder area to assist in lowering the hips gently to the mat. Be prepared to spot the back straddle roll.

4. **Headstand to Knee Scale:** From a stag posed headstand (b) open the forward leg and extend it toward the mat (c). Place the weight on the toe (d), lower that knee to the mat, and push with the arms to lift the body up into a knee scale (e).

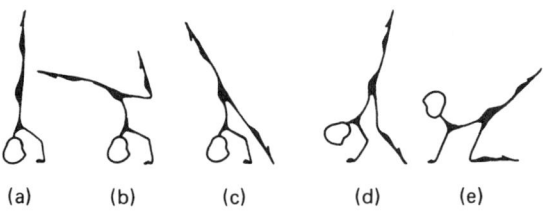

(a) (b) (c) (d) (e)

5. **Headstand Forward Roll:** From the basic headstand pike at the hips and place more weight on the arms; tuck the chin to the chest to initiate the rolling action. Push with the hands; then

inverted balances

reach forward and finish in a standing position or finish with any of the forward roll variations from Chapter 1.

Spotting: Once the student is in the headstand, move to a position facing the student's stomach. Holding on to the student's ankles, help the student pike by touching the student's stomach with your knee. Hold the ankles in place until the student has tucked the chin to the chest to initiate the roll. (Stabilizing the ankles as the body pikes assures the correct head position before the roll starts. If the student mistakenly lifts the head up and tries to roll, this safety measure will prevent injury to the neck.) As the forward roll progresses along the spine, give the ankles a gentle push to add the momentum needed to arrive in a standing position. Any forward roll variation out of the headstand could be used.

6. Headstand to Forearm Balance: [Use the forearm balance (page 58) for a progression.] From the headstand position (a) readjust the hands by moving them closer to the ears so that the entire forearm can be placed on the mat (b). (The forearms should be parallel to each other.) The back will arch as the forearms are moved into position (c). Lift the head and move the shoulders upward and toward the elbows. Continue pressing with the fingers and arch the back to move into the basic forearm balance (d).

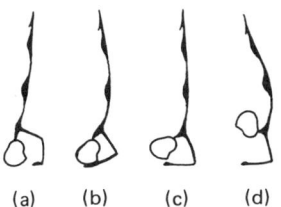

(a) (b) (c) (d)

7. Headstand to Handstand Progressions: Handstand balance (page 62) and the following exercise: Execute the headstand position with the feet against the wall and the head close to the wall (a). Push with the arms as the feet slide upward on the wall toward the ceiling to help in drawing the body into the handstand position (b). (The spotter can assist by grasping the hip area during the headstand and reminding the student to push and lift the hips into the handstand balance.) [Students will try to keep the

inverted balances

feet in place on the wall and merely arch the back during the push into the handstand (c and d). This is incorrect. The feet must slide upward on the wall to assume a handstand with little back arch.] Repeat this progression several times and work up to 5–10 repetitions. You are now ready to practice the skill away from the wall support.

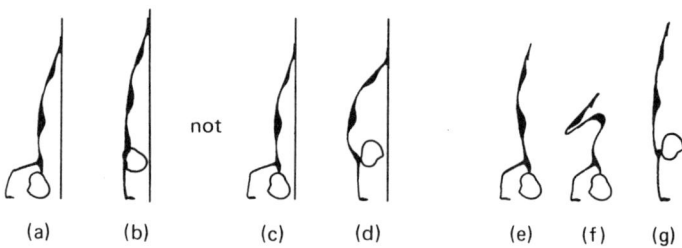

(a)　(b)　not　(c)　(d)　(e)　(f)　(g)

To add momentum to the movement, lower to a tuck position (f) while in the headstand balance. Then to get up into the handstand, thrust the legs to extension as the arms push (g).

FOREARM BALANCE
(Elbow Stand)

Progression: From a forward stride, deep lunge position with the *hips held high,* the forearms placed on the mat, the palms down, the fingers spread, and with the hands and arms parallel (a), execute several switch kicks while pushing downward from the shoulders. Kick up the rear leg followed by the front leg; change the leg position so that the rear leg will return to the mat first in the forward stride position, the second leg taking up the rear position of the lunge. Repeat. As students work on this progression, give verbal cues to press with the hands, elbows, and shoulders and to keep the shoulders high.

St. Pos.:   Same as (a) above.

Sk: Init.:   Attempting to keep the shoulders *high and over* the *elbows,* kick up the rear leg (b) and then the front leg. The back is arched, and the head is up as the legs are quickly joined together (c). Keep the shoulders from falling downward toward the wrists. Fingers press to hold balance; step down one leg at a time.

(a) (b) (c)

Spotting: Stand on the rear leg side of the student facing the student's shoulder area. As the rear leg kicks upward, grasp the thigh with both hands and, if necessary, lift to a balanced position. Encourage the student to remain tight and to push down with the shoulders. If the shoulders begin to fall forward, use your knee to return them to the correct position. *Do not* let the student arch over into the back bend position during the first trials. Have the student step down from the balanced position one leg at a time.

Variations:

1. Forearm Balance to Knee Scale: From the basic balance open the legs to a stag position (a). The straight leg must arch over the head to counter balance this stag position. Extend the flexed leg and place the toe on the mat (b). Support the body weight and continue to kneel on that leg (c) and push with the arms to assume the knee scale position (d).

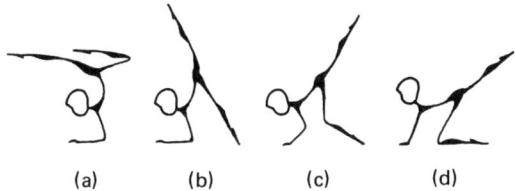

(a) (b) (c) (d)

2. Forearm Balance Pose Positions: See pose diagrams for the headstand balance on page 55. Add to those posed positions

inverted balances

the following: both legs bent with the toes to the head; one foot to head and the other leg extended in the basic forearm balance position; yogi position with straight legs; yogi position with tucked legs; yogi position with one leg straight and one leg bent.

3. Forearm Balance to Forward Roll: From the balanced position pike at the hips and tuck the chin to the chest to initiate the forward roll. The hands must push hard to move the hips into the roll position.

4. Forearm Limber: From the balanced position arch over into a back bend and then stand up out of the back bend position. (As the feet contact the mat in the back bend, the arms straighten and the hands thrust off of the mat and quickly reach overhead to assist in the stand.

5. Forearm to Back Bend Pose: From the balanced position maintain the forearm position on the mat as the legs arch over to the back bend position. The following poses may be used.

Return either by executing an inside-out action (page 78) or by kicking over to step down out of the forearm balance.

6. Forearm Balance to Chest Stand: This skill is for students who have limber backs. From the forearm balance (a) slide the elbows outward (b), lower the chin (c) and chest to the mat (d),

inverted balances

and balance in a chest stand. The final hand and arm position depends on the amount of back flexibility (e, f, g, or h).

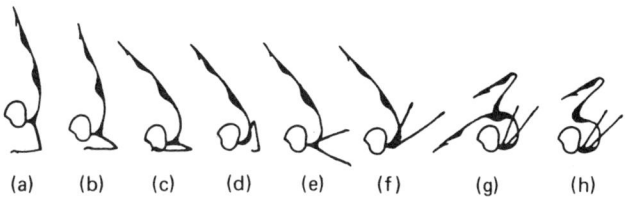

(a)　(b)　(c)　(d)　(e)　(f)　(g)　(h)

7. Once the student can consistently kick up and maintain the forearm balance, the skill can be made more difficult by balancing (a) and then lifting the hands one at a time to an under the chin position (b). Balance is maintained on only the elbows (c).

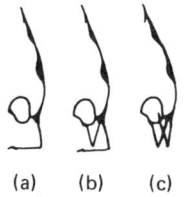

(a)　(b)　(c)

8. Hand-Forearm Balance: The starting position is similar to the forearm stand, except that only one forearm is placed on the mat and the other arm is extended sideways at shoulder level with the palm placed on the mat. From this position practice supporting the body weight by doing some switch kicks as described in the forearm balance progression. Kick into the balance as if doing the basic skill. Most of the weight is supported on the forearm with the other hand pressing firmly against the mat. [As the students learn this skill, the leg position can be changed to any pose described on pages 55 and 60. The student can return to a knee scale as described in variation (1) or a forward roll as described in variation (2).]

9. Forearm Balance, Walkover to Split: From the balanced position open the legs to a split position and begin the walkover

inverted balances

action by bending the leg that would contact the mat first. Place that instep in the mat as the hips press forward and upward and the body is lowered to a split. The student must have a limber back to do this skill.

HANDSTAND

Progressions: Start in a forward stride lunge position with the hands placed on the mat *directly* below the shoulders, the *arms straight,* the *shoulders extended,* the fingers spread and pointing forward, and the head up.

    1. Execute several switch kicks. The teacher gives verbal cues to the student to push downward with the shoulders during the kicking action so that the body weight is supported on the hands. Keep the head up so that you will not kick over into a back bend.

    2. From the starting position above kick up the rear leg and then the forward leg. Quickly join them momentarily in the air and then step down one leg at a time. (Explain to the students that they are not to kick upward with much force; it is not desirable at this time to get to the handstand position. This progression is to program the students to support the body weight momentarily on the hands with the shoulders extended as the legs are kicked upward and joined together without involving the possibility of falling over into a back bend.)

    3. Handstand with Spotters: From an erect standing position step forward and place the hands on the mat with the shoulders extended and the arms straight; kick upward into the handstand balance. The legs are quickly joined firmly together and the back is as straight as possible.

Spotting: Stand facing the student's side. As soon as the near leg kicks upward, grasp the thigh with both hands. Give verbal cues to press the legs together, to push out with the shoulders, and to stay tight; stretch the near leg upward to remove the arch from the back. Quickly attempt to balance the student in this extended position and line the hips up over the shoulders and the shoulders

inverted balances

over the hands. (If the shoulders are out of position, adjust them with your knee.) As the student tires, the shoulders will sink and the back will arch. Do not keep the beginners in the handstand position too long because they will become so tense that they will hold their breath and tire quickly. If the student is having difficulty kicking up to the handstand, grasp the thigh of the rear leg before this leg kicks upward; then help lift the student into the handstand while reminding the student to push with the shoulders. Do not allow students to walk forward on their hands as they kick upward. (Walking forces the spotter to support the total body weight.) Continue to hold onto the student during the step-down out of the handstand. Slow down the action by placing one arm around the stomach as one leg is lowered.

4. Handstand Against Wall: Place the hands approximately 1 foot from the wall and kick the legs upward. Push with the shoulders and allow the feet to touch the wall. Keep the shoulders extended and the arms and legs straight so that only the toes contact the wall. The entire foot should not touch the wall. Press with the fingers and lift the head. If the body is straight and tight, this action will pull the toes away from the wall.

5. Yogi Handstand Against Wall: Place the hands from 6 to 8 inches from the wall and kick upward to a handstand position. Place the feet against the wall (a). Pike the body and press the hips and legs against the wall (b). Drop the head and place the chin on the chest (c and d). As the shoulders move away from the wall, continue to pike at the hips by lowering the legs toward the face (e). If the hands are the correct distance from the wall for the individual, once the legs are piked, a pressing action with the finger tips will move the hips away from the wall into a free balance.

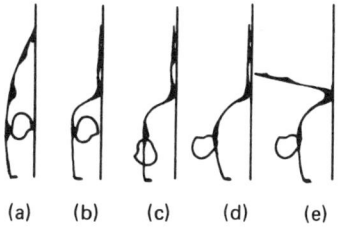

(a)   (b)   (c)   (d)   (e)

As students learn the yogi balance with the help of the spotters and the wall, they can practice kicking into the balance on their

inverted balances

own. If they remember to kick upward with the shoulders already extended, quickly joining the legs together reaching to the ceiling with the toes to straighten their backs, they should be able to maintain their balance before piking into the yogi position.

Spotting: Grasp the near thigh with both hands. Place your elbow in the hip area to force the pike; tell the student to drop the head and place the chin on the chest. Balance the student by gently positioning the shoulders with your knee.

HANDSTAND POSES

1. German handstand: Drop the head to a neutral position; body is completely straight (a).
2. Stag pose (b).
3. Double stag (c).
4. Split pose (d).
5. Split, rear leg flexed with foot to head (e).
6. Tuck (f).
7. Legs flexed with feet to head (g).
8. Yogi (h).
9. Stag yogi (i).
10. Tuck yogi (j).
11. Overbalance (k).
12. Stag overbalance (l).
13. Stag control overbalance (m).
14. Split control overbalance (n).

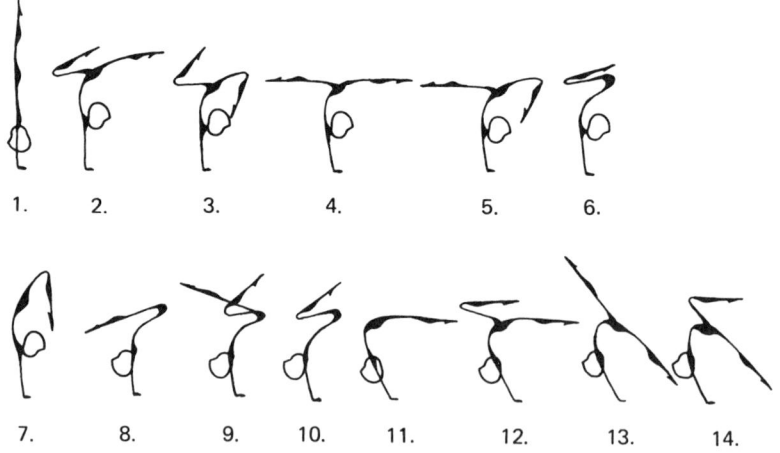

VARIATIONS MOVING OUT OF THE HANDSTAND BALANCE

The following variations begin with the basic handstand balance.

1. Step down. As the first foot contacts the mat, execute a one-half turn toward the extended rear leg. The arms must press off the mat forcefully and then reach overhead as the student steps forward onto the free leg.

2. Press with the shoulders and slowly lower one leg to the mat into a Swedish fall position. Move out of it by arching the back and crossing the extended leg over the supporting leg into a split position, or as the extended leg rotates over the body, bend the supporting leg to finish in a deep lunge position.

3. Slowly pike the legs downward while pressing with the shoulders; stand.

4. Slowly pike the legs downward while pressing with the shoulders. Toes contact the mat with the ankles extended. Bend the knees into a kneeling position.

5. Straddle the legs, press with the shoulders as the hips tuck under, and lower the feet to the mat in a straddle stand. (The feet should be placed on the mat in line with the hand position.)

inverted balances

6. Same as (5) except straddle through to a straddled L position or a straddle sit. Then move backward into a roll variation shown in Chapter 1.

7. Arch over into a back bend pose (page 77).

8. Arch over into a limber or limber variation (page 81).

9. Open the legs to a split position and arch over into a walkover or into a walkover variation (page 83).

10. Gently lower to forward roll.

Spotting: Stand facing the student's side and grasp the near thigh. Press your elbow into the student's hip area to force a pike position. Gently lower the student into a pike balanced position on the back of the neck and shoulders. Have the student hold this momentarily to feel the landing position for a controlled roll from the handstand balance. Gently press on the ankles to assist the student in continuing the rolling action.

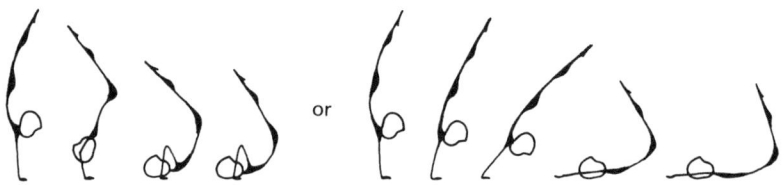

11. Straight Arm Forward Roll: Keep the arms straight and lead forward from the shoulders. Just before the face nears the mat tuck the head and pike the body. Then the roll begins. Any forward roll variation can be used out of the handstand roll.

12. Lower to Forearm Balance: Lower the elbows one at a time or simultaneously to the mat. The back increases the arch as the elbows contact the mat.

13. Lower to Headstand: This can be used as a progression for the backward handspring to the headstand balance. Lower the head to the mat gently as the body extends toward the arms.

14. To Split: Open the legs to the split pose. Press off the mat with one arm pivoting over the other arm and drop into the split. One hand is always in contact with the mat; the hips land next to the supporting hand. Pressing off and dropping into the split position are similar to a cartwheeling action. To finish in a

inverted balances

split with the right leg forward, the right leg should be toward the chest during the handstand split pose.

15. Snap-Down: This is a progression for the backward handspring (not to be confused with a "mule kick"). As the student kicks into the handstand, the shoulders and arms prepare to shove off the mat. The legs remain straight and together as they begin to whip downward. The hands and arms thrust the body into the air and rotate about the frontal axis. As the legs descend, the arms are vigorously thrown upward followed by the head and chest. Just before the landing the knees bend slightly to prepare for the explosive punch needed for the rebounding jump. When practiced correctly this skill is similar to the last half of the backward handspring. The important phases of this skill are the shoulder thrust, the arm lift and throw to the overhead position, and the explosive rebounding jump out of the snap-down.

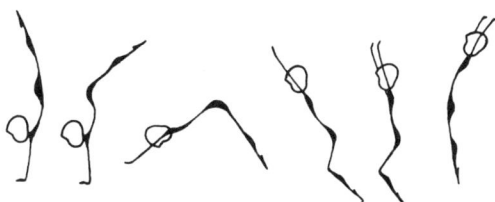

16. Walking on the Hands: This is easier than maintaining the static balance. Assume the handstand position, and then keep the back as straight as possible slightly overbalance; this forces the center of gravity outside of the forward edge of the base. As this occurs, take a step with the hands. [Once the students learn how to walk forward on the hands, they can begin to practice walking in circles, in curved patterns, following lines on the floor, walking backward, and walking sideways (similar to sliding sideways on the feet)]. Practice walking a square by taking 6 steps forward, 6 steps to the right, 6 steps backward, and then 6 steps to the left.

17. Walking with Split Kicks: Kick the legs to split positions with each hand movement. As the right hand moves forward, move the left leg overhead to the split position; as the left hand moves forward, kick the legs to a split position with the right leg overhead. There is a leg kick with each hand movement.

inverted balances

18. Jumping: From the handstand position bend the knees and kick the legs toward the ceiling as the arms and shoulders thrust off the mat. Immediately upon landing, bend the knees again to prepare for the next jump and thrust off again. Repeat the continuous jumping action and progress in a straight line or in a circle.

19. Pivot and Roll: From the balanced handstand position twist the body one-half turn. As the elbows bend, lower the back of the head to the mat for the roll. Do not move the hands from the initial handstand position. The twisting action causes the arms to cross as the elbows bend lowering the head to the mat.

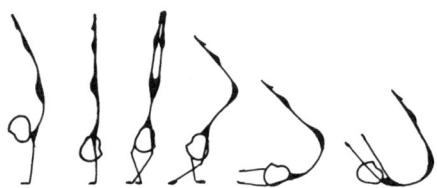

VARIATIONS INTO THE HANDSTAND POSITION

1. Cartwheel to handstand.
2. Half Turn into Handstand: Stand erect with the weight on the left leg, the right leg forward, the right arm raised overhead, and the left arm out to the side. Step forward onto the right leg, rotate the right hand inward and place it on the mat in line with the right foot; kick the legs upward (one at a time) as the right shoulder extends to support the weight; at the same time swing the left arm across the chest to initiate the turning action on the right arm; place the left hand on the mat next to the right in the handstand position. Step down out of the handstand or use any of the basic variations moving out of the handstand positions as explained above.

Spotting: Stand to the side facing the student's right shoulder. As the student kicks and pivots, grasp the left thigh and help to complete the turn. If necessary, assist in maintaining the student's balance. (By throwing the left arm harder and delaying its placement on the mat a full turn can be executed into the handstand balance.)

inverted balances

3. Handstand from Kneeling Position: Kneel on the mat; sit on the heeels with the arms extended overhead. Place the hands on the mat and lift the hips upward. Shoulders are moved slightly forward of the hands (arms remain straight) as the legs extend and force the hips above the hands. The toes are the last to leave the mat just as the hips are positioned above the hands. Students can execute this move through a pike position or a straddle as well as the tuck position.

Spotting: Stand facing the student's side where the handstand position will be executed. If necessary, position the hips. Grasp the near thigh to assist in balancing; be ready to adjust the shoulders with your knee.

4. Press to Handstand: Assume a straddle stand with the hands placed on the floor *slightly* forward of the feet. The arms are straight and the shoulders are slightly forward of the hands. Rise up on the toes and lift the hips over the hands; press down with the shoulders. When the hips are in the correct position and only the toes remain on the floor, the students will feel that they are going to fall onto their faces. This is the time to continue pushing downward with the shoulders, lifting the hips upward as the toes are lifted off the mat by straddling the legs (not jumping off the feet). The legs remain in the straddle position as the hips rotate upward into the position for the handstand. Once the hips are in place, the legs are lifted upward and pressed together.

Spotting: Stand in the forward stride position facing the student's back. Place your forward knee under the student's shoulder; reach over the hips and place your hands on the inside of the student's thighs. As the student is in the position to lift the toes off the mat, pull the hips and press on the shoulder with your knee. Position the hips and then maintain your grip on the student's thighs as you tell the student to join the legs together in the handstand. Reverse the procedure by straddling the student's legs. Give the cue to tuck the hips under as you pull on the legs and press your knee on the student's shoulder. Attempt to keep the hips over the hands during the straddle down to the starting position. You can also maneuver the student to a straddle-through to a straddle-L position. In order to return the student to the handstand balance from the straddle-L position retain the grip on the thighs and lift the student's hips to a position over their shoulders through the pressing action explained above.

ADDITIONAL INVERTED BALANCE VARIATIONS

ADDITIONAL INVERTED BALANCE VARIATIONS

ADDITIONAL INVERTED BALANCE VARIATIONS

3
back bends

BACK BEND PROGRESSIONS

Push-Up into Back Bend

St. Pos.: Assume position (a) with the feet apart, the hands under the shoulders, and the elbows pointing to the ceiling.

Sk. Init.: Straighten the arms and legs and lift the hips upward and toward the feet; as the hips are raised, drop the head between the arms and lift upward to look toward the feet. Try to straighten the arms and the legs while in the back bend position.

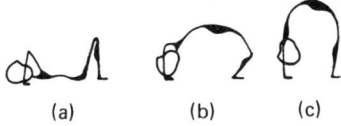
(a) (b) (c)

Spotting: Assistance is necessary to show the student how to push downward from this peculiar starting position. Give verbal cues, telling the student to stand heavily on the legs (beginners tend to attempt to support the body weight on only the arms), push downward with the arms, and drop the head so that the hips can rise (if the head is in the wrong position and the chin is on the chest, the hips tend to sink downward). Assist by lifting under the back with one arm and lifting the near shoulder with the other hand. Once the position is reached, encourage the student to continue the pushing and standing action. Then assist the student in lowering gently to the starting position on the mat.

Rock in the Back Bend Position

St. Pos.: Same as (a) above.

Sk. Init.: Push up into the back bend position as described above; then attempt to completely straighten both the arms and the legs (b). (If the arms are not extended, the student will probably lower the head to the mat during the rocking action.) The rocking action is initiated by the legs pushing against the mat causing the hips and shoulders to move forward as in (c). The hips and shoulders reverse the action by forcing the hips over the feet (d). Repeat the rocking action forward and backward to stretch and to gain momentum.

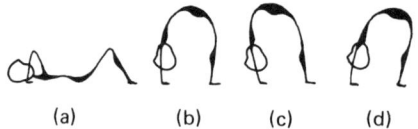

(a)   (b)   (c)   (d)

Rocking Back Bend with Arm Thrust

St. Pos.: Assume the back bend position with arms and legs extended (a).

Sk. Init.: Initiate the rocking action as explained above. As momentum is gained and as the hips move over the feet (b), extend the arms forcefully (c); make an effort to stand as the hands are momentarily lifted from the mat (d). Replace the hands

back bends

quickly (e) so that the forward phase of the rocking action will take place (f). Repeat the arm thrust each time the hips are moved over the feet. Continue rocking in the back bend with the arm thrust several times. (This gives the students the kinesthetic awareness of the technique needed to stand up out of the back bend position.)

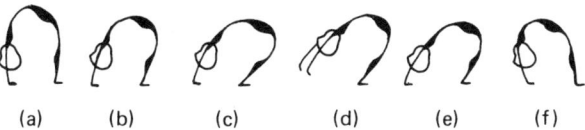

(a)   (b)   (c)   (d)   (e)   (f)

Back Bend with Spotting

St. Pos.: Stand with the legs shoulders width apart and with the arms extended overhead. [Spotter stands facing the student in a forward stride position and grasps the hip area (a)].

Sk. Init.: The spotter cues the student to arch the back and look for the mat while reaching for the mat. The spotter usually has to offer encouragement at this point and as the arching action takes place assist by positioning the hips over the student's feet to insure that an arching action instead of a leaning action takes place (b). The spotter remains ready to assist in the lowering action but continues to encourage the student to do most of the work (c). During the last 8 inches of lowering into the back bend, the spotter reminds the student to reach for the mat and attempt to push against it before the hands actually contact the surface (d). The spotter should offer support during this time as well as when the hands contact the mat in case the student forgets to continue pushing with the arms. As the position is stabilized, the spotter releases the student to balance.

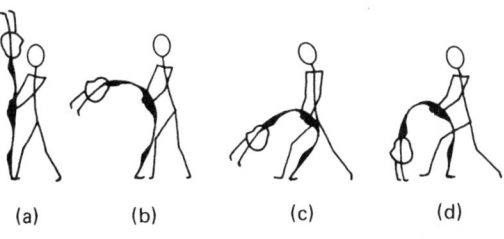

(a)   (b)   (c)   (d)

back bends

Recovery: The spotter remains in the forward stride position with hands grasping the student's hips (a). A rocking action is initiated with the spotter's assistance. The spotter rocks the student toward the hands (b) and then toward the feet (c). The spotter repeats the rocking action toward the hands (d) and then tells the student to stand as the weight is moved over the feet (e). It is important that the student use the arms to thrust off the mat and then reach overhead (f and g) to stand up out of the back bend position.

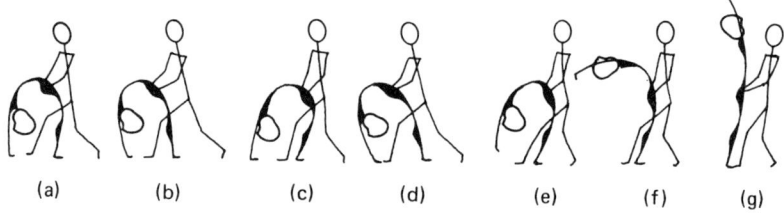

(a) (b) (c) (d) (e) (f) (g)

Rocking Back Bend with Leg Thrust

St. Pos.: Assume the back bend position with arms and legs extended (a).

Sk. Init: Initiate the rocking action as explained on page 74. As momentum is gained and as the hips move over the hands (c), extend the legs forcefully (d); make an effort to hold an overbalanced handstand position by lifting the legs to a position parallel to the mat (e); replace the feet so that the forward phase of the rocking action will take place (f and g). Repeat the leg thrust each time the hips are moved over the hands. Continue rocking in the back bend with the leg thrust several times. (This gives the students the kinesthetic awareness of the technique needed to execute the backward limber variations.)

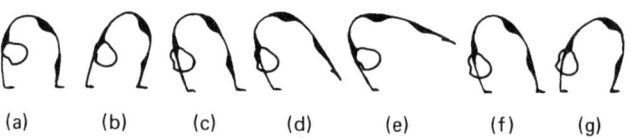

(a) (b) (c) (d) (e) (f) (g)

back bends

Pose Positions for the Backbend

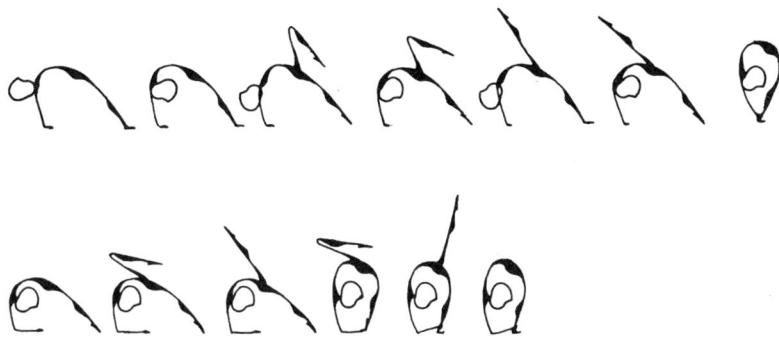

WALKING IN THE BACK BEND POSITION

St. Pos.: Assume the basic back bend position.

Sk. Init.: A walking action is initiated by moving the feet in toward the hands and then moving the hands outward. This feet-in, hands-out action is repeated as the student progresses headfirst down the length of the mat.

Spotting: Assistance may be needed to show the student the direction of the movement. Support the lower back, if necessary, as cues are given to move the feet in. It may be necessary to manually move the student's arms in the outward movement.

Variations:
   1. Progress down the length of the mat with the feet leading. To do this, move the hands in toward the feet and then move the feet outward. Spotting may again be necessary to indicate the desired direction of the movement.
   2. A sideways sliding movement may be used by reaching out to the side with the right arm and right leg and then moving the left arm and left leg in the same direction. Continue the sliding movement across the length of the mat. Reverse the action to return to the starting position.
   3. Rotating Back Bend: Move the right arm to the right

back bends

and the left leg to the left. Then move the left arm to the right and the right leg to the left. Take small steps and then reverse to return to the starting position.

PONY KICKS

St. Pos.:   Assume the basic back bend position (a).

Sk. Init.:   While in the back bend a prancing action takes place with the legs. One knee is tucked toward the chest (b) and then extended so that the leg is pointing to the ceiling (c) this leg is lowered to the back bend position while the other knee is tucked upward (d) and kicked to the ceiling (e); the prancing action continues.

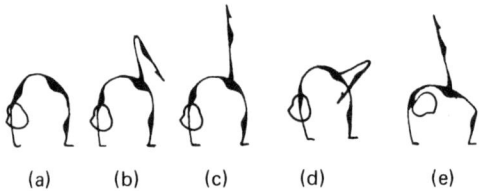

(a)   (b)   (c)   (d)   (e)

Variation:
   The prancing action takes place as the student walks in the back bend position (feet first) down the length of the mat.

INSIDE-OUTS

St. Pos.:   Assume the basic back bend position (a) crosswise on the mat.

Sk. Init.:   The following explanation describes the technique used to rotate toward the right side: The left arm is lifted from the mat and raised across the chest as the body weight is supported on the legs and right arm. As this left arm approaches the mat, the left leg shoves off the mat. The left hand contacts the mat and

back bends

the left leg is crossed over the right. The student is now in a prone, all-fours position. From this position the *right leg* is lifted and then crossed over the left, rotating the hips; the right arm thrusts off the mat and the body rotates to the back bend position. The student must keep this right arm extended over the head and focus on the hand in order to assume the back bend position.

Spotting: Be in a position so that the student will rotate toward you. Place one arm under the student's back during the back bend position. Touch the student's left arm and tell the student to raise it across the chest. Slight support is given to position the center of gravity over the new base (one arm and both legs). As the student's hand contacts the mat, give the cue to lift the left leg and cross it over to the prone position. Now tap the student's right leg and tell the student to lift it upward and over the left leg. As the foot contacts the mat, tap the right arm and tell the student to lift it and keep it overhead as the eyes are focused on the hand. Slight support is given as the student rolls over into the back bend position. The student must straighten the hand position and then continue with another set of inside-outs.

Since this is an excellent stretching exercise, it is important that the student execute the skill both toward the right side and the left side.

Variation:
Student can execute the inside-outs in a circle by taking small steps with the hands and larger leaping steps with the legs as the rotation is made from the back bend position into the prone position.

FRONT LIMBER

Progressions: Kinesthetic awareness of the stretched handstand position and the ability to stand up out of a back bend position.

St. Pos.: Stand with the weight supported on one leg; extend the dominant leg forward with the toes contacting the mat. Extend the arms overhead (a).

Sk. Init.: Lift the forward leg (b) and step into the handstand position with the shoulders extended (c), the legs joined together (d), the back straight, and the ankles extended. The shoulders pull back as the legs are slowly lowered to the mat to a back bend position (e and f). The ankles must extend with the toes reaching for the mat in order for the student to execute a smooth standing action out of the backbend. The feet should be kept close together (do not allow the student to open the legs to a wide straddle position for the back bend). At this time the hips move forward and upward as the arms, hands, and fingers press off the mat reaching quickly overhead (g and h).

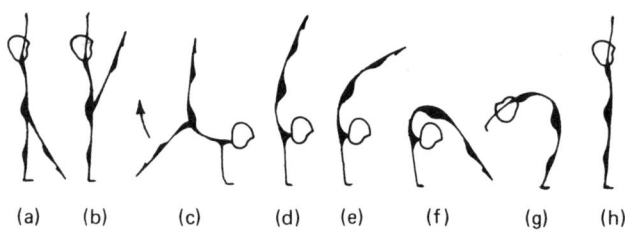

(a)   (b)   (c)   (d)   (e)   (f)   (g)   (h)

Spotting: Follow the directions for spotting the handstand balance (page 62). As the student begins to arch over, place both arms under the student's back so that the student will slowly lower the feet to the mat. Once the student is in the back bend position, allow the student to adjust the feet for comfortable support without help. Have the student rock in the back bend in order to gain momentum to stand. Readjust the hands by placing one arm under the small of the student's back and the other hand on the student's upper arm. As the weight is moved over the feet, press the hips forward and upward and lift the upperarm while giving the student verbal cues to thrust off the mat and stand.

Note: The limber should be done smoothly and with control; the student should not fall into the back bend position.

back bends

Variations:

1. In order to encourage control and stretch, practice this skill keeping the hands close together (hooking the thumbs). Place the feet close together as soon as they reach the handstand position.

2. Limber to Kneeling Position: Once the stretched handstand balance is reached, bend both knees and keep the legs joined together. Move the shoulders toward the heels of the hands. Arch the back and lower the pointed toes and insteps to the mat. As the toes contact the mat, move the hips forward and upward as the arms, hands, and fingers press off the mat and the knees lower to the mat. Finish in an extended kneeling position. Follow this skill with a side roll variation (page 42) or move from the kneeling position into either a forward roll or handstand variation.

3. Half Turning Limber: Kick upward into the handstand position with one arm turned outward. As soon as the legs are joined together, thrust one arm off the mat and initiate a one-half turn; then replace the arm to the mat in a handstand balance. Do any of the variations listed for moving out of the handstand balance (see page 65).

4. Full Turning Limber: Kick into the handstand position with one arm rotated outward. As the legs join together, thrust the straight arm off the mat. This causes the body to rotate about the turned-out arm. As the hand is replaced on the mat to the opposite side of the supporting hand, thrust that hand off the mat. This causes the body to rotate again. Replace the hand in the handstand position as the second one-half turn is completed. Recover through any of the variations listed on pages 65–68.

back bends

5. Limber from Knees: Kneel in an extended position with the arms overhead (a). Lower the upper body and place the hands on the mat (b) as the legs extend lifting the hips upward toward the handstand position (c). Extend the shoulders as the hips lift to the handstand position (d). The legs are straight by now. Kick the heels forcefully to the extended handstand balance (e). Arch over to complete the limber (f).

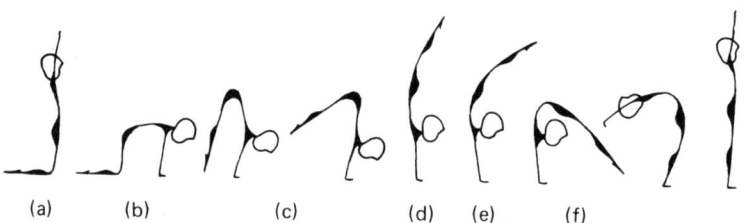

(a) (b) (c) (d) (e) (f)

6. Arabian Limber: Stand with the legs straight and together. Extend arms overhead (a). Bend the knees slightly as the torso pikes forward. Place the hands on the mat (b). At this time extend the legs forcefully (c) and thrust the hips upward into the handstand position (d). Either tuck the legs (e and f) and extend them upward to the handstand or keep them straight as the heels are kicked to the handstand. Once in the stretched handstand position, arch over and slowly lower the feet to the mat to complete the limber.

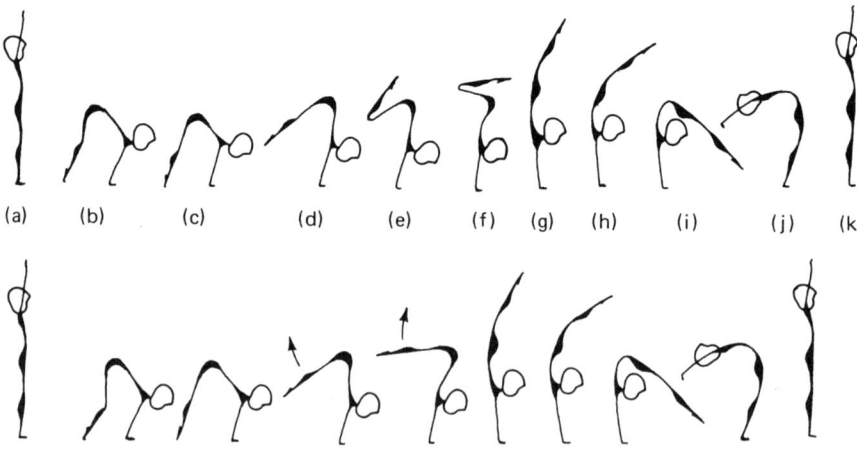

(a) (b) (c) (d) (e) (f) (g) (h) (i) (j) (k)

back bends

FORWARD WALKOVER

Progression: Forward limber with the feet held close together during the landing and standing phase.

St. Pos.: Stand on one leg with the dominant leg forward, ankle extended, and the toes contacting the mat. Extend the arms overhead (a).

Sk. Init.: Lift the forward leg (b) and step into the skill as if going into a handstand (c) position with the ankles extended. During the split handstand balance, move the shoulders toward the heels of the hands, arch the back and lower one leg toward the mat (e). Keep the head upward in a position to look for the landing leg to contact the mat. Keep the legs straight as one contacts the mat, toes first (f). Move the hips forward and upward as the heel is lowered to the mat. Tighten the thigh and thrust off the mat with the arms. Reach the hands and fingers (g) quickly upward with the arms so that they finish in an overhead position (h). Stand on only the supporting leg; extend the other leg forward and upward; then lower the extended leg to the mat and step forward onto that leg.

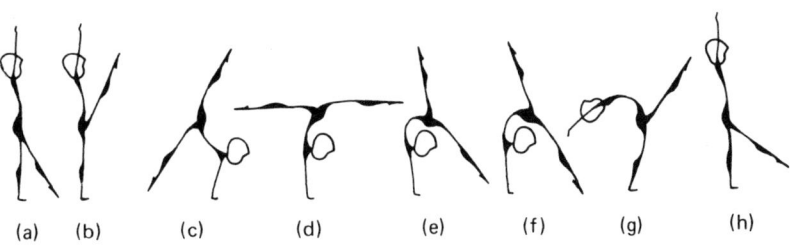

(a) (b) (c) (d) (e) (f) (g) (h)

Spotting: Stand to the side of the forward leg and in the direction of where the handstand position will take place. As the split handstand position is reached and the shoulders move back, place your arm around the small of the student's back; place the other arm under the extended leg. As the student attempts to stand, press the hips forward and upward with the arm around the student's back and extend the free leg forward and upward with the arm that is under that leg. (You can control the walkover action

back bends

by controlling the free leg. As you reach under the leg, position your upper arm under the calf area and bend the arm so that the fingers can reach over the top of the thigh. In this position it takes a minimum of effort to assist in extending this leg to the finish position.)

Note: The shoulders should be completely extended during this skill. The elbows and the legs do not bend. The beginner often bends the knee of the landing leg in an attempt to get it closer to the hands. When the hips move forward, they go beyond the area of the base and the student falls to the knee. Another common error is to land only on the toes; the heel must contact the mat for the stand. The landing foot should be centered so that it contacts the mat directly between the two hands, not off to one side. If the student pulls the chin to the chest during the brief back bend phase of the skill, the action will sink the hips and force the supporting leg to bend; it will not be possible to stand smoothly.

Variations:

1. Once the student can do the basic forward walkover, the student should strive to execute this skill showing as much leg amplitude as possible. The stand should occur with the free leg high in the air. The spotter can assist by spotting the forward walkover as explained above; however, the spotter must keep the extended leg high as the student thrusts off the mat, reaches overhead, and grasps the ankle of the extended leg with both hands. The student then pulls this leg close to the face while keeping both legs completely straight. The spotter will have to assist in balancing the student during this stretch.

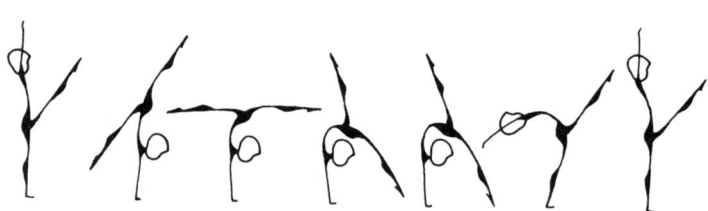

back bends

Students should practice the walkovers with the dominant and then the nondominant leg leading.

2. To encourage shoulder control and stretch, have the students execute this skill holding the hands close together during an entire series of walkovers. This should be practiced on a line drawn down the center of the mat. This is a progression for the forward walkover on the balance beam and also for the one arm walkover.

CONTROL FORWARD WALKOVERS

Progression: Forward walkover with shoulder extension.

St. Pos.: Stand in a low scale position on the dominant leg with the chest and head up and with the arms extended back toward the hips (a).

Sk. Init.: Raise the extended leg upward. This causes the chest to be slowly lowered so that the hands can be placed on the mat with the shoulders extended (b). The free leg continues to arch over into the split handstand position as the supporting leg is lifted from the mat because of shoulder extension (c). Shift the shoulders as the back arches and one leg is lowered to the mat (e and f). Extend the free leg forward and upward as the arms, hands, and fingers thrust off the mat and reach quickly overhead (g and h). Stand only on the supporting leg. Lower the free leg to the mat and step into another low scale position to repeat the controlled walkover (a).

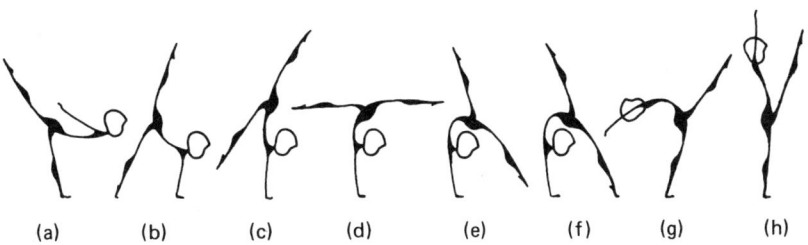

(a)　(b)　(c)　(d)　(e)　(f)　(g)　(h)

back bends

FORWARD KICK WALKOVER

Progression: Forward walkover and control walkover.

St. Pos.: Assume a position to execute *either* the basic walkover (page 83) or the controlled walkover (page 85).

Sk. Init.: Move into the split handstand position with the shoulders completely extended. Attempt to show total amplitude in the split position and in the ankle extension (a). From this position bend the dominant leg quickly so that the foot slaps the thigh of the extended leg (b); immediately straighten to the split position (c) and complete the walkover by shifting the shoulders and lowering the base leg to the mat (d). Practice this skill on both the dominant and nondominant sides.

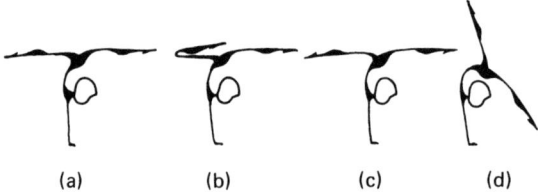

(a)   (b)   (c)   (d)

Variations:
1. Use this for a balance beam progression by keeping the hands close together during the skill and by working on a straight line drawn down the middle of the mat.
2. Practice doing a controlled walkover starting from the low scale position.
3. Finish this skill in a split position (see the technique description on page 90).

FORWARD DOUBLE KICK WALKOVER

Progression: Forward kick walkover and control walkover.

back bends

St. Pos.: Be ready to execute either the basic walkover or the control walkover.

Sk. Init.: Move into the split handstand position with the shoulders extended. Show total amplitude in the split position and in the ankle extension (a). From this position bend the dominant leg and open it quickly so that the foot slaps the thigh of the extended leg as in the kick walkover (b); bend the extended leg and straighten it quickly so that the foot taps the top of the head (c). As the legs return to the split handstand position (d), continue the walkover action (e). Practice this skill on both the dominant and nondominant sides.

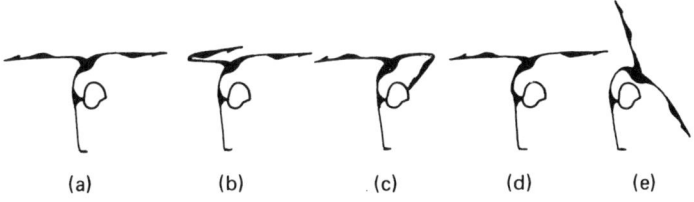

(a) (b) (c) (d) (e)

Variations:
1. Practice this skill by keeping the hands close together during an entire series of double kick walkovers.
2. Once the leg action is learned, practice using the technique for the controlled walkover.

FORWARD CABRIOLE WALKOVER

Progression: Forward walkovers; control walkovers and the carbriole kicks as described here: From a V-sit position on the mat, hands on mat next to hips, rotate the legs outward at the hip, hold them in a stride position so that one is slightly crossed over the other. Using a quick closing then opening action, slap the legs together so that they *contact* each other at the *calf area*. The legs must remain straight. This cabriole kick is used in the walkover.

back bends

St. Pos. and Sk. Init.: The starting position and the skill initiation are as for either the basic or the controlled forward walkover. Once the split handstand position is reached (a), execute the cabriole kick (b). Open the legs quickly to the starting split position (c) (the legs do not change positions). Then shift the shoulders and complete the walkover action (d). Practice on both the dominant and nondominant sides.

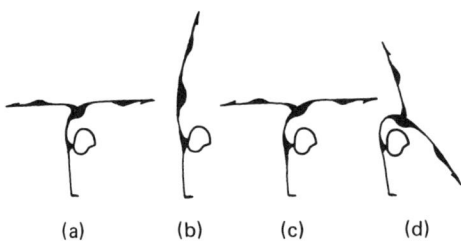

(a)   (b)   (c)   (d)

Variations:

1. Practice this skill by keeping the hands close together as if working on the balance beam.
2. Finish the walkover in the split position by following the directions on page 90 after the cabriole kick.

FORWARD SCISSOR WALKOVER

Progression: Forward walkovers on both the dominant and nondominant sides.

St. Pos.: Be ready to execute either the basic walkover or the controlled forward walkover.

Sk. Init.: Move into the split handstand position with the shoulders extended. Show total amplitude in the split position and in the ankle extension (a). As this position is reached, forcefully kick the legs to reverse positions in the split handstand (b). Once again show total amplitude in this new split handstand.

back bends

Then shift the shoulders and complete the walkover action (c).

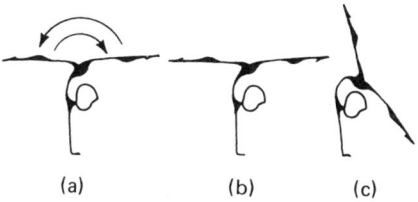

Variations:

1. Practice the skill as if working on the balance beam. Keep the hands close together.

2. Practice this skill on both the dominant and nondominant sides.

3. Once the leg action is learned, use a control walkover for this skill.

4. After doing the one-leg scissor, do another scissor and finish the walkover standing on the dominant side. Finish this skill by assuming a split position (see page 90).

5. Follow the directions described in (a) through (b) in "Sk. Init." Then assume the double stag position (shown below) before completing the skill.

PARTNER FORWARD WALKOVERS

Progression: Forward walkovers.

St. Pos.: Students stand side-by-side with arms extended overhead. Two, three, or more students can execute this skill. The

back bends

partners who have shorter arms grasp the wrists of the partners who have longer arms.

Sk. Init.: The line of partners step into the walkover at the same time as the hands are placed on the mat (if only two partners are doing this skill, three hands will contact the mat; one hand will be on the partner's wrist). The basic walkover technique is used. During the arm thrust phase the partners who are holding wrists try to press off the mat and help in lifting the arms quickly to the overhead position at the finish of the skill.

Variations:
 1. As the students perfect the timing of doing the basic walkover together, have them try some of the walkover variations: kick, double kick, cabriole, scissor, spotters, swing-throughs, and walkovers to split positions. The different walkovers can be alternated as the students progress down the length of the mat and finish in the walkover to split.
 2. One or more of the partners can be doing backward walkovers while the others are executing forward walkovers.

FORWARD WALKOVER TO SPLIT POSITION

Progression: Forward walkover; split position.

St. Pos.: Be ready to execute either the basic walkover or the control walkover.

Sk. Init.: Move into the split handstand position with the shoulders extended. Show total amplitude in the split position and at the ankles (a). As the shoulders shift in order to lower the first leg to the mat (b), bend this leg at the knee (c), pull the foot toward the head and place the foot on the mat with the ankle extended (d). Place weight on the toes and instep as the hips move forward and upward and the arms press off the mat (e) (by this time the knee has been lowered to the mat and the

back bends

extended leg is still reaching forward and upward.) Keep the back arched and the head back as the hips move forward to lower to the split position (f). As the split position is reached, extend the body upward so that the torso can lean forward to a pose position (g).

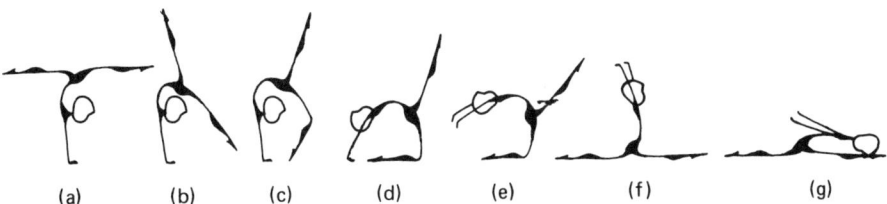

(a) (b) (c) (d) (e) (f) (g)

ONE-ARM WALKOVER

Progression: Walkovers with the hands held close together.

St. Pos.: Be ready to execute either the basic walkover or the control forward walkover.

Sk. Init.: Place one hand on the mat. Swing the other arm by this supporting arm while passing through the split handstand position. Shift the shoulders as usual and lower one leg to the mat as the free arm is reaching upward toward the ceiling. The free arm continues the reaching action as the stand takes place; by this time the supporting arm is also reaching upward to an overhead position.

Practice alternating the left and then the right arm while progressing along the length of the mat. The shoulders must be extended.

Practice on the nondominant side as above.

Variations:

1. Practice on a line as if working on the balance beam.

back bends

2. Execute any of the following forward walkovers on one arm: kick, double kick, cabriole, scissors, walkover to split.

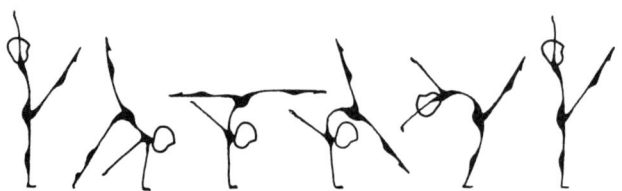

ONE-ARM CONTROL WALKOVERS

Progression: One-arm walkovers to the dominant side using the opposite arm. (If the student executes the forward walkover with the right leg forward, the student should use the left arm for this particular variation.)

St. Pos.: Stand on the nondominant leg (the left leg) with the right leg extended upward, the right hand grasping under the knee. Extend the left arm overhead so that it is ready to begin the skill (a).

Sk. Init.: Hold onto the right leg with the right arm and step down with the right foot as the left leg is being lifted backward and upward (b) into the split handstand position (c). Continue to hold the right leg with the right arm and use the left hand as the support arm (d). Continue the walkover to the stand phase while the right hand is still holding onto the right leg (e and f).

Practice on the dominant and nondominant sides.

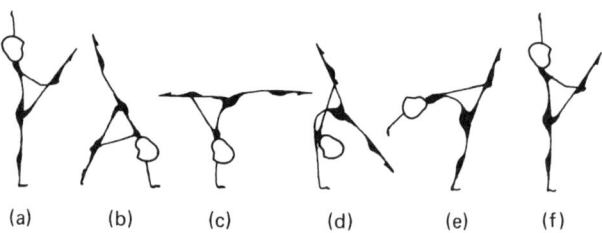

(a)　(b)　(c)　(d)　(e)　(f)

Variation:
   Practice the one-arm control walkover in series moving smoothly down the mat.

FORWARD WALKOVER ON CANE OR BATON

Progression: One-arm walkovers; any of the walkover variations using only one arm for support: kick, double kick, cabriole, scissors, and walkover to split.

St. Pos.: With the preferred supporting arm for the one-arm forward walkover grasp the shaft of the cane (baton) near the base. Keep this arm straight. With the other hand grasp near the middle of the shaft. This arm is used to stabilize the implement and the arm remains bent.

Sk. Init.: Step into the walkover and place the base of the cane (baton) on the mat while kicking the rear leg into the handstand position. The bent arm holds the implement steady as the second leg is lifted from the mat. Once the handstand position is reached, shift the shoulders. Keep the bent arm close to the chest and lower the first leg to the mat. As this foot comes in contact with the mat, thrust off the mat with the implement and reach quickly overhead. Now repeat the skill.

Variation:
   Once the students have learned to execute the forward walkover while holding onto the cane (baton), present other variations of this skill: kick, double kick, cabriole, scissors, and the walkover to the split position.

ONE-ARM PARTNER WALKOVERS

Progression: One-arm walkovers using either arm.

St. Pos.: Partner A will do the walkover while partner B assists. They then change positions and partner B does the walkover while partner A assists. The following description is for walkovers starting with the *right leg forward* using the *left arm* for support: Partners stand side-by-side; partner A bends the right arm and holds it across her stomach while the left arm is extended overhead. Partner B takes hold of this right hand in a handshaking position with her right hand. They are now ready to begin. (Reverse this position if the partners wish to use the right arm for support.)

Sk. Init.: Partner A extends her left arm and steps into the one-arm walkover by leaning over the grasped hands. She places the left hand on the mat and kicks into the walkover. As the stand from the walkover occurs, both arms will be overhead as well as the right arm of Partner B. Partner A now steps left in front of Partner B who takes a small step to the right, then reaches overhead with her left arm, and is in the starting position as described above. Partner B executes the one-arm walkover. At the completion of the skill her arms will be extended overhead and she will step to the left in front of Partner A who takes a small step to the right. This alternation of one-arm walkovers is continued down the length of the mat.

CHASING WALKOVERS

Progression: One-arm walkovers to the dominant side using that same arm. (If the student executes the walkover with the right leg forward, the right arm must be used for support.)

St. Pos.: Be ready to begin the one-arm walkover. (This particular skill series will move the student around in a circle.)

Sk. Init.: Execute a one-arm walkover leaning to the right; during the recovery to a standing position, instead of lifting the arms up overhead, keep the right arm to the right side of the body and continue to reach downward toward the floor as the right arm swings sideways into position for another walkover. (Each walkover is done in the leaning position and each walk-

back bends

over gets faster and faster as the student continues to reach for the floor during the recovery phase.) As the lean and the speed of the walkovers increase, hold the right arm within inches of the floor when it is not supporting the body weight. After executing several of these chasing walkovers, step forward, reach upward, and spin in order to assume a balanced standing position.

SPOTTING FORWARD WALKOVERS

Progession: Control forward walkovers.

St. Pos.:   Be ready to execute either the basic walkover or the control walkover.

Sk. Init.:   Execute the forward walkover and land on one leg; extend the other leg forward and upward. Lower this extended leg downward, swing it back past the supporting leg, and take a large backward step onto this leg. Lift the supporting leg from the mat, swing it downward past the new supporting leg, and continue to swing backward and upward as the hands are placed on the mat in order to execute the next forward walkover. Continue this stand-up, step-back, swing-back into the next walkover several times without progressing forward on the mat. To be successful, reach overhead as the step-back occurs. Then use the backward lifting action of the next leg to lower the chest and hands to the mat. Do the series smoothly and in a controlled manner. Practice on both the dominant and nondominant sides.

Variations:

1. Once the students have learned to execute the series of walkovers in place, they can use any of the walkover variations: kick, double kick, cabriole, and scissor.

2. It is possible to do the spotting walkovers moving sideways on the mat. These are called spiral walkovers. The student merely steps obliquely backward to either the left or right side and then swings through to the next walkover. Again, the arm lift and reach are important in successfully completing the skill.

back bends

BACKWARD KICKOVER

Progression: Back bend.

St. Pos.: Back bend position; push up to this position or arch backward to it from a standing position (a).

Sk. Init.: Kick one leg upward (b) and push with the shoulders as the other leg jumps off the mat (c) and lifts overhead through the handstand position (d). Keep the legs in the stride or split position during the handstand and step down one leg at a time.

Note: This is a skill many students try on their own once they can hold the back bend position. It is not to be confused with the backward walkover. This kickover skill is difficult to execute because there is no momentum to begin the kicking action from the starting back bend position. The advantages of the kickover skill for the beginner are that the beginner (1) feels more secure using the large base (both feet and hands are on the mat) and (2) can adjust the starting position until ready to kick upward into the skill. The backward walkover is a smoother action.

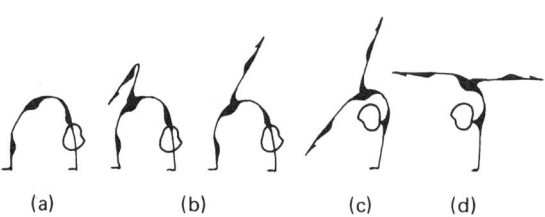

(a)   (b)   (c)   (d)

BACKWARD WALKOVER

Progression: Back bend from standing position (page 75).

St. Pos.: Stand in the forward stride position (dominant or kicking leg forward) with weight on the rear leg, forward leg straight

back bends

with ankle extended, and toes in contact with the mat; extend the arms overhead.

Sk. Init.: With the aid of a spotter, arch backward and look for the mat. Before the hands contact the mat, extend the shoulders attempting to push the body away from the mat. As the hands contact the mat lift the forward leg upward; then jump off the supporting leg and lift it upward overhead to the handstand position (there is a great deal of shoulder extension at this time). Keeping the legs in the stride or split position, continue to push away from the mat with the shoulders. Lower one leg and then the other leg to the mat as the arms press off and reach overhead.

Spotting: Stand facing the student's shoulder area and on the side of the forward kicking leg. Place one arm around the small of the student's back so that the hand can hold the ribs; place the other hand under the thigh of the forward leg. As the student arches backward, looking for the mat with the arms overhead, give verbal cues reminding the student to push away from the mat with the shoulders and to lift the forward leg. Assist in lifting this leg to the handstand position as the hips and shoulders are positioned by the forearm of the arm that was around the student's back. (This arm first assisted in lowering the hands gently to the mat; it now positions the center of gravity over the base by pushing on the student's back toward the direction of the skill; there is no grip change.) If the student's shoulders fall forward, you can reposition them with your knee. Once the lead leg has been raised to the handstand position, remove the hand on that thigh. There is no need to throw this leg downward to the mat. Beginners tend to close the legs together during the handstand phase of this skill; if this is a problem, you can prevent this by grasping the following leg as the step-down action begins. Students must extend at the shoulders and push away from the mat before the hands contact the mat. If they wait to push with the shoulders, the elbows will bend as the body weight is transferred to the arms and the students will fall on their heads. It is important that the students learn the shoulder control in this skill. Once the handstand position has been reached, the shoulders move to the

back bends

step-down side of the hands and continue to push away from the mat.

BACKWARD WALKOVER
TO A SWEDISH FALL POSITION

Progression: Backward walkover.

St. Pos.: Forward stride position with the weight supported on the rear leg, the forward leg straight, the ankle extended, the toes in contact with the mat, and the arms extended overhead (a).

Sk. Init.: Execute a backward walkover to the stride handstand position (b). The hips remain over the hands, shoulders slightly toward the finger tips, head up legs straight and in the stride position. The shoulders press downward as the toes and instep of the lead leg are slowly lowered to the mat, the following leg remains extended upward in a Swedish fall position (e).

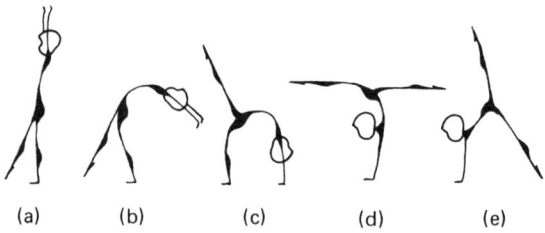

(a)   (b)   (c)   (d)   (e)

Variations:

1. Execute the backward walkover to a Swedish fall position holding the hands close together as if working on the balance beam. This is a progression for the control work needed on the beam and for one-arm backward walkovers.

2. From the Swedish fall position cross the extended leg over the base leg by arching the back and pushing off the mat with one arm to execute a one-half turn. Pivot over the base foot and one arm and lower the extended leg to a split position with the base leg forward.

3. Same as (2) above, but during the pivot *bend the base leg*. This forces you to finish in a deep lunge position with the Swedish fall base leg forward and the arm in contact with the mat.

4. From the Swedish fall position bend the base leg and lower that knee to the mat. At the same time lift the head to a knee scale position.

5. Same as above, but lower the hips and the extended leg to the mat in a half split position. Arch the back, bend the rear leg, and lift the foot to the head.

CONTROL BACKWARD WALKOVER

Progression: Backward walkover to Swedish fall position (page 98).

St. Pos.: Stand with the dominant leg extended at waist level, arms raised overhead (a). (The extended leg can be bent at the knee if it is difficult to hold the starting position; the ankle is extended.)

Sk. Init.: As you arch backward into the walkover, lift the extended leg toward the face (b). Extend the shoulders as the base leg is raised from the mat and the body passes into the handstand position (c). Keep the hips over the base with the shoulders slightly forward so that you can lower one leg to the Swedish fall position (d); then stand on the foot keeping the following leg extended high in a scale position (e); press the hands and arms off the mat and extend toward the hips to hold the final scale position.

Spotting: Assist in balancing the student in the starting position by following the directions for the backward walkover spotting.

Note: Students should practice this controlled walkover to both the dominant and nondominant sides. The arms and legs should remain completely straight and the shoulders and ankles extended. Total amplitude should also be demonstrated in the split position of the legs. This skill should be practiced with the hands held

back bends

close together as if working on the balance beam. Using this small base takes complete shoulder control.

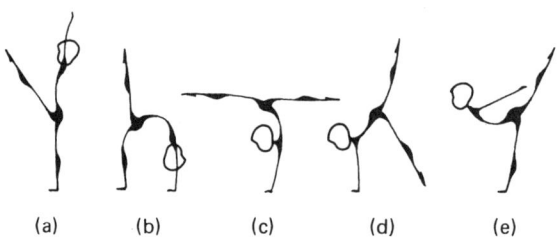

(a)   (b)   (c)   (d)   (e)

BACKWARD KICK WALKOVER

Progression: Backward walkover.

St. Pos.:   Be ready to execute a backward walkover or a control backward walkover.

Sk. Init.:   After the lead leg is lifted to the split handstand position (a), bend that knee so that the foot slaps the other thigh (b). Immediately straighten the leg to the split handstand position (c); continue to finish a controlled backward walkover (d). Practice on both the dominant and nondominant sides.

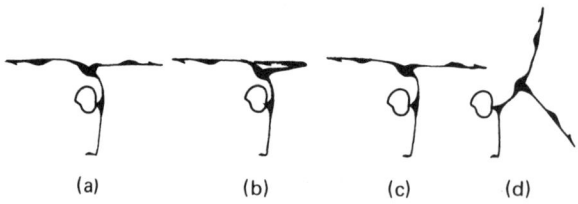

(a)   (b)   (c)   (d)

Variation:

From the split handstand position after the leg kick recover through any of the variations listed for the backward walkover to the Swedish fall position, page 98.

back bends

BACKWARD DOUBLE KICK WALKOVER

Progression: Backward kick walkover (page 100).

St. Pos.: Be ready to execute a backward walkover or a control backward walkover.

Sk. Init.: Begin with the action explained in the backward kick walkover. As soon as the lead leg kick is completed (a–c), bend the second leg so that the foot taps the top of the head (d). Immediately straighten the leg to the split handstand position (e) and step downward as in the controlled backward walkover (f).

Practice on both the dominant and nondominant sides.

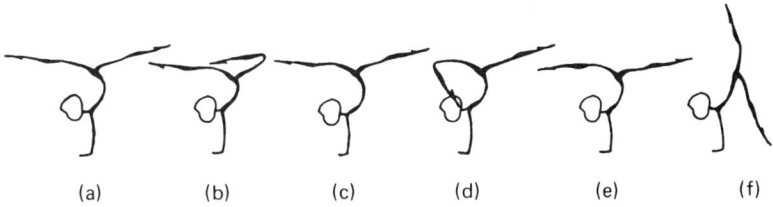

(a)   (b)   (c)   (d)   (e)   (f)

Variations:

1. After the double kick has been completed, recover to any of the variations listed on page 98 for the backward walkover to the Swedish fall.

2. If you have good control in the handstand position, a leg scissor can take place after the double kick has been completed.

3. You would then step down to the mat in a controlled manner or use any of the variations listed on pages 98–99.

BACKWARD CABRIOLE WALKOVER

Progression: Backward walkover and cabriole kicks: Sit on the mat in a V-sit position, rotate the legs outward at the hip, and hold them in a stride position so that one is slightly crossed over the other. Using a quick closing and then an opening action, slap the legs together so that they contact each other at the calf area. This cabriole action is then executed in the backward walkover.

Sk. Init.: Execute a backward walkover to the split handstand position (a). Do the cabriole kick (b) and return the legs to the split handstand position (c). Then step downward in a controlled manner (d). Practice this on both the dominant and nondominant sides.

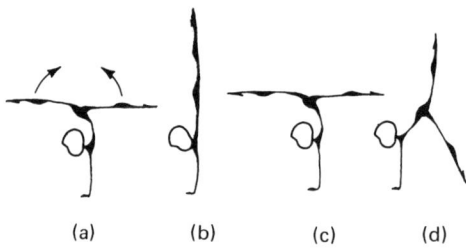

(a)   (b)   (c)   (d)

Variation:

Recovery can be made through any of the variations listed on page 98.

BACKWARD SCISSORS WALKOVER

Progression: Backward walkover on both the dominant and nondominant sides.

St. Pos.: Be ready to execute the basic walkover or the controlled backward walkover with the dominant leg forward.

Sk. Init.: Execute the backward walkover to the split handstand position (a). At this point the legs forcefully kick to change positions in the split handstand (b). (Before this scissor action takes

back bends

place total amplitude should be shown in the split handstand.) Step down to the mat in a controlled manner (c). Practice on both dominant and nondominant sides showing total amplitude in the shoulders and the ankles, and in both split positions.

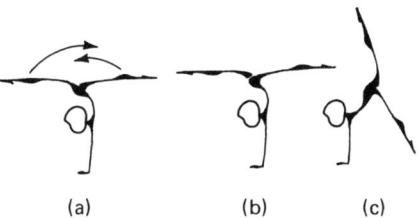

(a)   (b)   (c)

Variation:
Any of the variations on page 98 can be used for recovery phase of this skill.

ONE-ARM BACKWARD WALKOVER

Progression: Backward walkover with hands joined close together.

St. Pos.: Be ready to execute the basic walkover or the controlled backward walkover (a).

Sk. Init.: As you arch backward looking for the mat, place only one arm on the mat (b), lift the other arm and the head (c and d) to finish along side of the supporting arm at the completion of the skill (e.) (The shoulder must be completely extended before contacting the mat in order to support the body weight.) Practice this skill by alternating the left and right arms. Then practice it on the nondominant side alternating the left and right arms.

Spotting: Assist as indicated in the backward control walkover

back bends

on page 99. Give cues to extend the shoulder to reach upward with the free arm.

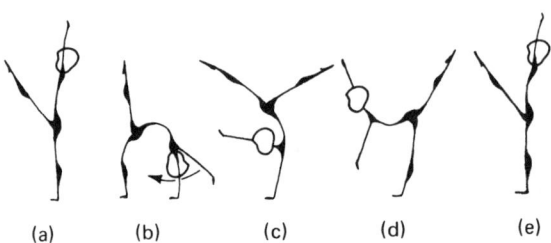

(a)   (b)   (c)   (d)   (e)

BACKWARD WALKOVER ON CANE OR BATON

Progression: One-arm backward walkovers.

St. Pos.:   With the preferred supporting arm for a one-arm backward walkover, grasp the shaft of the cane or baton near the base. Keep this arm straight. With the other hand grasp near the middle of the shaft. Use this arm to stabilize the implement and keep the arm bent.

Sk. Init.:   Arch backward and place the end of the cane or baton on the mat; hold it in a steady position with the bent arm as the legs kick over into the backward walkover.

Spotting: Assist as in executing the basic backward walkover. Take care to notice the shoulder position. If the shoulders fall forward of the baton base you can reposition them with your knee.

Variations:
Once this skill is learned, other walkover variations can be used: kick, double kick, cabriole, scissor, spotters and walkover to split.

SPOTTING BACKWARD WALKOVERS

Progression: Control backward walkover.

back bends

St. Pos.: Be ready to execute a controlled backward walkover.

Sk. Init.: Lift the dominant leg into the split handstand position. Press the shoulders against the mat as the dominant leg is lowered to the mat. Thrust the arms off and reach upward as the following leg swings past the supporting leg. Take a big step forward. Now swing the dominant leg forward and upward as the arms reach overhead. This allows you to execute another walkover. (The step-down, step-forward, swing forward, and reach to go into another spotting walkover is repeated for each spotting walkover. The series should be done smoothly and in a controlled manner.) Practice on both the dominant and nondominant sides. Since this skill can be used on the beam, practice the spotting walkovers keeping the hands close together.

Variations:

1. Once this skill is learned, use any of the walkover variations: kick, double kick, cabriole, and scissor.

2. It is possible to do the spotting walkovers moving sideways on the mat. These are called *spiral walkovers:* As the first landing leg contacts the mat, swing the second leg forward and cross in front of the base leg. Place the second leg on the mat to support the body weight as the dominant leg swings forward into the next walkover. Spiral backward walkovers leading with the right leg will move across the mat to the right.

GAINING BACKWARD WALKOVERS

Progression: Spotting backward walkovers.

back bends

St. Pos.: Be ready to execute control backward walkovers.

Sk. Init.: Proceed as if doing spotting backward walkovers, but instead of taking a step forward to execute the next walkover in the same place, take a very large step using a leaping action. Then swing the dominant leg forward and upward to go into the next walkover. Progress forward down the length of the mat while doing backward walkovers.

SWING-THROUGH BACKWARD WALKOVER

Progression: Control backward walkover on the dominant and nondominant sides.

St. Pos.: Be ready to execute a control backward walkover.

Sk. Init.: Execute the control back walkover to the split handstand position. As the first leg contacts the mat, thrust the arms off the mat and reach forward and upward. Maintain balance on this supporting leg while swinging the nondominant leg past the supporting leg, lifting it upward as the hands reach overhead in order to go into another backward walkover on the nondominant side. (Again, only the first leg contacts the mat, the other leg swings past the supporting leg, lifts upward with the arms and the student executes another walkover. Dominant and nondominant side walkovers alternate as the student progresses down the length of the mat. Total amplitude should be demonstrated in the shoulders, ankles, and legs. This skill series takes a great deal of control. The arms must reach upward in order to insure a smooth swing-through action.)

Variation:
If you can only execute a control walkover using the dominant side, this series can be used along with a scissor walkover. Execute a scissors walkover, step down, and swing-through to another scissor walkover. Each take off will be on the dominant leg.

back bends

PARTNER WALKOVERS

Progression: Backward walkovers.

St. Pos.: Partners stand side by side with their arms extended overhead. The partner who has the shorter arms grasps the wrist of the taller partner. They are now in position to begin the skill. If three or more people are doing this skill, they form a chain. Each person holds onto the wrist of the person next to her.

Sk. Init.: The partners arch backward and go into the walkover. Only three hands will contact the mat; the one hand remains grasped around the partner's wrist. Any of the backward walkover variations can be executed in this manner (kick, double kick, cabriole, scissors, spotters, gainers, swing-throughs, or walkovers to split).

Variation:
One or more of the partners can be executing forward walkovers while the others are doing backward walkovers. Again, any walkover variation can be used: kick, double kick, cabriole, scissors, spotters, gainers, or swing-throughs.

BACKWARD WALKOVER TO SPLIT

Progressions: Controlled backward walkovers and split.

St. Pos.: Be ready to execute a controlled backward walkover.

back bends

Sk. Init.: As the handstand position is reached, keep the hips over the hands (a) and the shoulders slightly forward of the finger tips (b). Lower the forward split leg (c); then lift it slightly upward as the hands push to allow the leg to slip between the hands (d). Lower the hips gently to the mat in the split position. The hips will contact the mat between the hands (e).

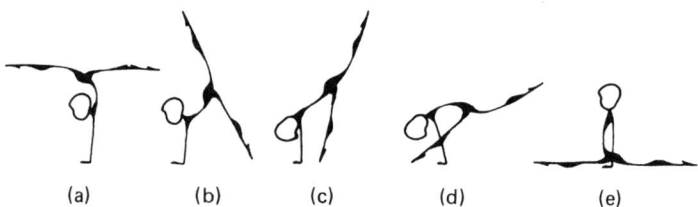

(a)   (b)   (c)   (d)   (e)

Variations:

1. If you are not flexible enough to pull through to this split position, slice the legs to the side to assume the split. Execute a backward walkover to the split handstand position. At this time lower the forward split leg just to the side of the arms rather than between them. Thrust the arm close to this leg off the mat as your hips drop to the mat in the split position next to the supporting arm.

2. Use the following walkover variations before moving into the split position: kick, double kick, cabriole, or scissor.

BACKWARD WALKOVER TO HANDSTAND BALANCE

Progressions: Backward walkover and handstand balance with variations.

St. Pos. Be ready to execute a backward walkover or a controlled backward walkover (a).

Sk. Init.: As you arch backward, lift the forward leg to a handstand position (toes pointed toward the ceiling) (b). The second

back bends

leg follows joining the first leg in the stretched handstand balance (c). Keep the back straight and the shoulders and ankles extended (d). Step downward one leg at a time.

Spotting: Stand to the side of the student where the handstand balance will take place. As the first leg approaches the handstand position, grasp that thigh with both hands and balance the student. Give verbal cues to join the legs together and push with the shoulders.

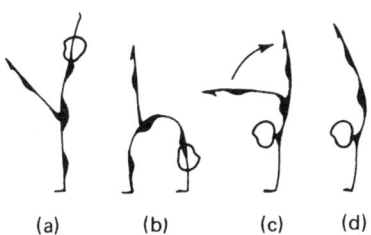

(a) (b) (c) (d)

Variation:
Make the recovery through any of the variations listed on pages 98 and 99 or through any of the variations listed from the basic handstand balance on pages 64–68.

HALF TURNING BACKWARD WALKOVER

Progressions: Backward walkover to handstand (page 108) and handstand balance on page 62.

St. Pos.: Be ready to execute the basic backward walkover with the arms extended overhead and one arm rotated outward from the shoulder.

Sk. Init.: Arch backward. Lift and then join the legs together in a handstand balance with the back straight, the shoulders and ankles extended, and the one arm and hand turned outward from the shoulder. As soon as the balanced position is reached, thrust one arm off the mat so that the body turns about the rotated arm. The arm that initiated the one-half turn by thrusting off the mat is replaced in a handstand position to the opposite side of the supporting arm. Step down one leg at a time or use any of the variations on pages 65–68.

Spotting: Stand on the side of the rotated arm. As the student lifts the legs to the initial handstand position, grasp the near thigh with both hands; balance the student and give verbal cues to join the legs together and then thrust off the mat into the turn. During the turn maintain the grip on the near thigh and help to pivot the student over the supporting arm by placing the center of gravity over that arm and walking through the turn in order to reposition the student in the second balanced handstand position. Then allow the student to step down in a controlled manner.

FULL TURNING BACKWARD WALKOVER

Progression: Backward walkover with half turn (page 109).

St. Pos. and Sk. Init.: The starting position and the skill initiation are identical to that listed before. Perform the backward walkover with the one-half turn; then execute another one-half turn by thrusting off with the last supporting arm and continue to stay in the handstand balance while the body rotates about the new supporting arm to finish the entire full turn. Either step downward one leg at a time or use any of the variations out of the handstand listed on pages 65–68.

If the student prepared for this skill with the right arm turned outward, then once in the handstand position, the left arm would first thrust off the mat so that the body would rotate about this right arm; as soon as the left arm is replaced on the mat to the opposite side of the right arm, the body stretches upward and toward the left arm as the right arm thrusts off the mat continuing to turn the body in the same direction. At the completion of this turn the student can recover from the stretched handstand balance through any of the variations listed before.

back bends

Spotting: Spotting is identical to that described in the half turning backward walkover with the additional one-half turn. Line the hips over the second supporting arm and again walk the student around to the new handstand.

BACKWARD ARABIAN LIMBER

Progressions: Backward walkover with variations.

St. Pos.: Stand with the legs together and straight and with the arms extended overhead (a).

Sk. Init.: Arch backward and look and reach for the mat (b). Just as the hands contact the mat, forcefully extend the ankles and thrust the feet from the mat (c). Extend the shoulders and lift the feet upward into a stretched handstand position (d). Keep the hips over the hands as the legs are piked downward in a controlled manner (e–g). (Often the students will never reach the stretched handstand position. Instead, they will jump off the mat into an overbalanced handstand position and then execute a mule kick action to recover from this arched handstand position.)

Spotting: If the student can do a backward walkover, you are needed mainly to help the student jump upward off the mat while keeping both legs together. To do this, kneel on one knee placing it near the student's heels. The other foot is placed on the mat with the knee turned outward so that the student will not fall onto the spotter's leg. From this position you are low enough to assist in executing the leg action and then can raise upward into a standing position on the other foot in order to position the legs or hips if necessary. Place one arm around the student's lower back and the other arm under the ankles. As the student arches backward, give verbal cues to reach for the mat and then jump; you will have to lift the legs slightly until the student gets the feeling of the timing of this skill. You should follow the student's body through the stretched handstand position and then be ready to reposition the shoulders with the closest knee. Using the arm that was around

112   *back bends*

the student's back, make sure that the hips do not fall forward causing the student to return to a back bend position.

Note: This skill takes back flexibility, a great deal of timing, and shoulder extension.

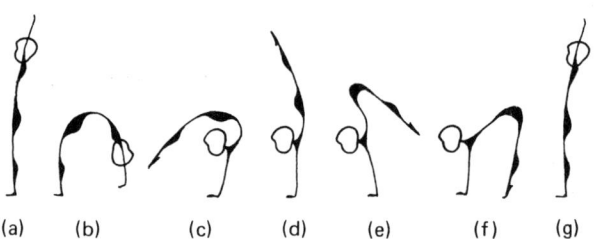

(a)   (b)   (c)   (d)   (e)   (f)   (g)

Variations:

1. Recover from the handstand position through any of the variations listed on pages 65–68.

2. If you are flexible and strong, the starting position can be changed to a kneeling position with the legs together and the arms extended overhead. Arch backward as the legs begin to straighten. Lift the knees from the mat so that the weight is supported on the *top* of the toes. Extend the shoulders as the toes are lifted upward to the handstand balance. Pike the legs down in a controlled manner to finish the skill. (This skill is called a "chucker.")

VELDEZ PROGRESSION

For a dominant right kicking leg assume the following starting position: Sit with the right leg completely extended on the mat, the left knee bent, the knee centered, and the left foot on the mat near the right mid-thigh area. Extend the left arm behind the hips with the hand in contact with the mat; extend the right arm obliquely forward and upward.

back bends

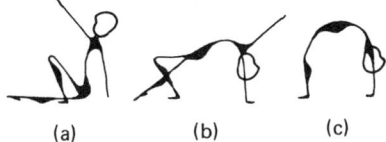
(a)　　　(b)　　　(c)

From this position (a) slowly lift the hips upward while supporting the weight on the left foot and hand (b). Drop the head back and look for the mat while placing the right leg in a back bend position (c). The right hand also contacts the mat in the back bend position. (This progression should be repeated several times so that the student can see the rotation of the supporting arm which is unique to this skill. The progression will also give the student the feeling of going straight backward into the back bend position, moving only in the sagittal plane.)

Veldez

St. Pos.: The starting position is as described above for the right dominant kicking leg. [Reverse for the left dominant leg (a).]

Sk. Init.: Prepare the extended right arm for the arm throw by lowering it slightly (a); then immediately throw it upward overhead (b) (not to the left side) as the right leg kicks upward and the hips lift upward as if going into the back bend position (c); extend the left leg at this time; then jump forcefully off the mat and lift upward to the handstand balance (d) as the right hand comes in contact with the mat to hold this balance. Then open the legs to the split handstand position (e) and step downward one leg at a time (f).

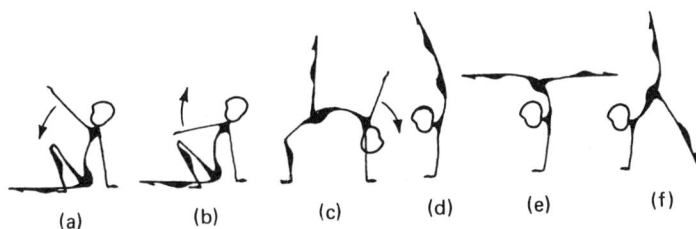
(a)　　(b)　　(c)　　(d)　　(e)　　(f)

back bends

Spotting: Kneel sitting on the heels facing the student's shoulder area on the side of the right arm which is extended obliquely forward and upward. Place the left hand on the back of the student's near hip and the right hand under the extended right thigh. (You must keep the face back out of the arm-throw path.) Give verbal cues to throw the right arm straight backward and directly overhead. Assist by lifting the hips with the left hand and lifting the kicking leg with the right hand. With the left hand push hard to position the hips in the handstand balance as you give cues to join the legs together. Your right hand releases the thigh area once the handstand position is reached; by keeping the left hand close to the hips during this balance you can be sure that the student will not fall back into the back bend position.

Variations:

1. Recover from the balanced handstand position (d) through any of the variations listed on pages 65–68.

2. *Veldez Walkover:* Execute a slightly slower Veldez action as described above, but have the right hand contact the mat *before* the left leg is lifted from the mat; keep the legs in a split position and finish as if doing a backward walkover.

3. *One-Arm Veldez:* The starting position and the skill initiation are described for the basic Veldez (not the Veldez walkover). The right arm throwing pattern is the same as for the Veldez (a–c), but that arm is not lowered to the mat; it continues reaching upward toward the ceiling in order to assist in the left shoulder extension (d). (This shoulder extension is important to the successful completion of the skill.) The legs remain in the split posi-

tion after the kicking phase and the student completes the step-down action as if doing a one-arm backward walkover (e).

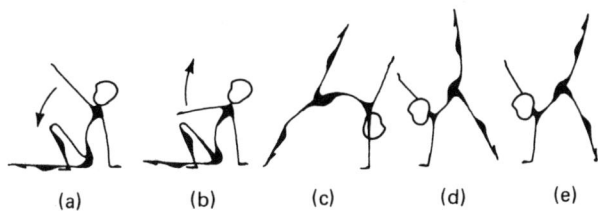

(a)　(b)　(c)　(d)　(e)

4. *Arabian Veldez:*

   Progression: Backward Arabian limber (page 111).

   St. Pos.: Sit with both knees bent, the feet on the mat, and the arms in position for a basic Veldez (a).

   Sk. Init.: Dip the right arm slightly downward and then immediately throw it upward overhead (a and b) as the legs begin to extend and the hips lift upward toward the ceiling (c). Thrust the feet off the mat (d) and while they are joined together, lift them upward to the handstand position while you place the right hand on the mat to balance this position (e). You can either step down one leg at a time (f) or you can recover from the handstand balance through any of the variations listed on pages on pages 65–68.

(a)　(b)　(c)　(d)　(e)　(f)

back bends

5. *Tinsica Veldez:* Be in position to execute the basic Veldez. The skill initiation is the same with the exception of the placement of the right hand, which is placed in a tinsica position rather than in the handstand position. Since this technique is used on the balance beam, it should be practiced on a straight line.

ADDITIONAL BACK BEND VARIATIONS

ADDITIONAL BACK BEND VARIATIONS

4
cartwheels

CARTWHEEL PROGRESSION

1. Switch Kick Handstand Progression: From a forward stride lunge position with the hands on the mat directly under the shoulders, the arms straight, the fingers spread and pointing forward, and the head up execute the switch kick action by kicking up the rear leg and then the forward leg. Change the leg position in the air so that the rear leg steps down first contacting the mat in the forward stride position. The forward leg now takes up the rear position. Repeat the kicks several times. Be sure to push downward with the shoulders. (This progression gives the students the kinesthetic awareness of the shoulder extension needed for the cartwheel as well as the feeling of supporting the body weight entirely on the arms. The kicks do not have to be very high. As the students are reminded to push downward with the shoulders, the kicking action will raise the legs higher and higher so that the inverted position is experienced.)

2. Practice the handstand position to remove the arch from

cartwheels

the back. Pay attention to the feeling of the straight handstand position. The muscles of the stomach must be tight and the toes must reach upward to the ceiling to accomplish the straight body handstand. [Use spotters (see handstand balance with spotters on page 62).]

3. If you have experienced the cartwheeling action, this progression may not be necessary. It is most helpful to know the feeling of doing a cartwheel on both the dominant and nondominant sides. (The progression impresses upon the student the necessary arm push and gives the experience of cartwheeling at a safe level.)

From a forward stride lunge position with the right leg forward pike the upper body downward and place the right hand just ahead of the right foot. Reach farther forward with the left hand and place it on the mat in line with the legs and the right hand. Push with the arms and shoulders as the rear left leg kicks around to land next to the left hand. The right leg jumps upward following the left leg. Lead back to the starting position by pushing with the arms and shoulders and kicking around with the rear right leg followed by the left. Continue kicking and jumping back and forth. Attempt to press down with the shoulders as you kick higher into the air. Soon the legs will pass through a completely vertical plane (there is no back arch). If you are pressing with the arms as the progression is repeated back and forth, momentum builds up and the arms are eventually lifted from the mat and you have to replace them for the next cartwheel.

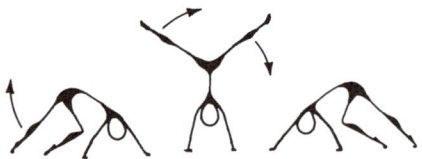

CONTINUOUS CARTWHEELS

Execute a basic cartwheel passing only through the vertical plane. There is *no* arch in the back. As the first foot contacts the mat, keep the second leg extended in the air. *Thrust* the arms off the mat and *quickly reach overhead* as the body executes a pivot toward the extended leg. You are now ready to repeat another cartwheel with a pivot progressing down the length of the mat. This movement should be smooth. There is no hopping action on the supporting leg during the pivot. The thrusting and reaching action of the arms assist in a smooth recovery from each cartwheel. Practice this skill series on *both* the dominant and nondominant sides, showing total amplitude in the shoulders and ankles, and in the straddle position. The emphasis is not on speed but on a slow, controlled movement. Try to place both the hands and the feet on a line drawn down the center of the mat.

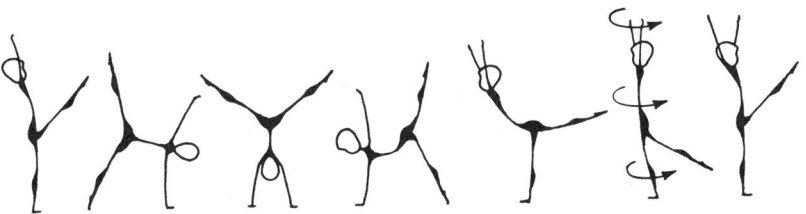

CONTINUOUS CARTWHEELS ALTERNATING LEFT AND RIGHT SIDES

Execute a continuous cartwheel to the right side, pivot and step forward onto the right foot. Swing and lift the left leg upward as the arms reach overhead to execute a left side cartwheel. Upon landing, step forward onto the left leg after the pivot. Then raise the right leg with the arms to go into the right side cartwheel. Continue to progress down the length of the mat alternating dominant and nondominant side cartwheels by stepping forward and then lifting the second leg to initiate the opposite side cartwheel. This series should be smooth and controlled. It should also show total amplitude in the shoulders, ankles, straddle, and leg lifting action going into the next cartwheel. Movement is only through the vertical plane. You should be placing both hands and feet on a line drawn down the center of the mat.

CARTWHEEL TO INWARD LUNGE

Execute a basic cartwheel to either the right or left side. Pull the first leg close to the hands, bend the knee as the leg contacts the mat, press the arms off the mat, and reach overhead as the chest lifts upward. This lifting action lowers the rear leg to the mat in a deep lunge position. (This is an inward turn since the student turns in toward the cartwheel.)

Note: The cartwheel to the inward lunge should be practiced on both the dominant and nondominant sides. As the student practices the skill, the ending arm position can be varied to different poses: hands on hips; one hand on hip and the other arm extended overhead; one hand on a shoulder and the other arm extended overhead; arms crossed in front of the chest; arms circled overhead; arms finish in opposition with the forward leg; etc.

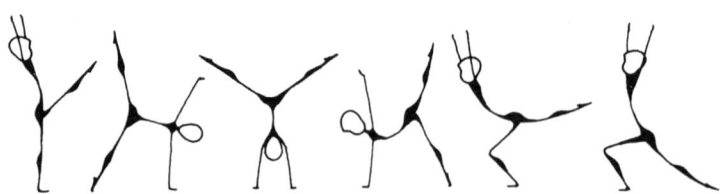

CARTWHEEL TO OUTWARD LUNGE

Execute the basic continuous cartwheel to either the right or left sides. Instead of beginning another cartwheel after completing the pivot, lower the extended leg into a lunge position. (This is an outward lunge since the student pivots away from the cartwheel and then lunges.)

CARTWHEEL WITH HANDS HELD TOGETHER

Continuous cartwheels are executed by holding the hands together (thumbs may be hooked) during the entire series of cartwheels. The hands should not separate at all as the student progresses down the length of the mat. This skill can be used as a progression for a one arm cartwheel since through its use it is possible to gain the feeling of supporting the body weight on a small base while using both arms. To develop complete control of the body and to encourage stretching the muscles equally, the skill should be practiced on both the dominant and nondominant sides. Total amplitude should be shown at the shoulders and ankles and in the straddle position.

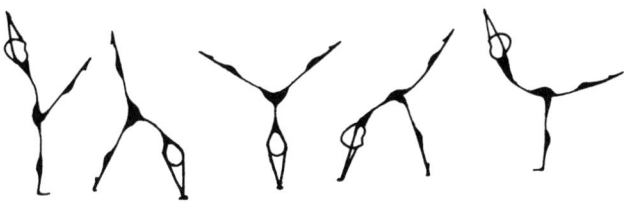

Variation:

Keeping the hands together, alternate right and left side cartwheels by finishing one cartwheel to the right side, pivoting to the right on the right leg, and then stepping left into the left side cartwheel. Continue alternating sides as the cartwheeling action progresses down the length of the mat.

CARTWHEEL FULL PIVOT TO BACK ROLL

Progressions: Cartwheel, cartwheel to outward lunge, backward roll variations from Chapter 1.

St. Pos.: Begin by preparing to execute a cartwheel to the dominant side (a).

Sk. Init.: Following the cartwheel rotate to the outward lunge as described on the previous page (b–e). The body immediately turns around, maintaining the lunge foot position by doing the following: rotate the upper body and then the hips toward the forward leg (f); support the body weight on this leg; continue the turn while lowering the hips to the mat in a sitting position with the forward lunge leg still bent and crossed over the rear lunge leg which is still straight (g and h). Quickly follow the turn to the sitting position by one of the backward roll variations (i).

(a) (b) (c) (d) (e) (f) (g) (h) (i)

CONTROL CARTWHEEL

Execute the basic cartwheel *slowly* and in a controlled manner so that the body weight is momentarily supported totally on the first arm to contact the mat (b) and then only on the other arm (c). Reach the free arm upward toward the ceiling. Keep the body completely straight, do not arch the back, and extend the shoulders. This skill takes control of the center of gravity and should be practiced on both the dominant and nondominant sides. It is a good progression for all variations of one arm cartwheels.

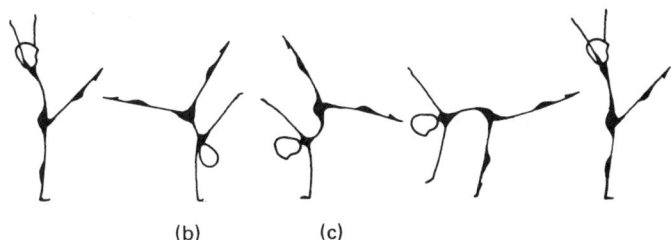

(b)   (c)

CONTROL CARTWHEEL
USING SCALE POSITION

This skill is excellent for teaching the pressing action from the shoulders, which is so important to the gymnast, but it is difficult to teach.

St. Pos.: From a low scale position with the arms extended by the hips (a).

Sk. Init.: Reach forward slowly with the arms and place the hands on the mat in the cartwheel position (b). Lift the rear leg upward to permit this action. Press the shoulders as the extended leg continues to lift upward through the cartwheel position (c). Place the body weight on the arms so that the supporting leg is lifted from the mat and into the cartwheel. Continue to press the shoulders as the supporting leg is slowly lowered to the mat while the extended leg remains high in the air (d); lift the head and chest upward to another low scale position (e). After holding this scale, return the hands to the mat to execute a controlled cartwheel on the nondominant side. Return to the starting scale position (e, d, c, b, a). Continue to work back and forth practicing the control cartwheels.

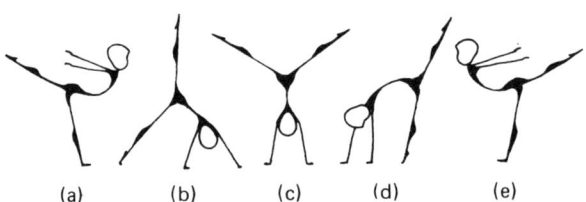

(a)　(b)　(c)　(d)　(e)

CONTROL CARTWHEELS USING SCALE POSITION PROGRESSING DOWN LENGTH OF MAT

St. Pos.: Low scale position with arms extended by hips (a).

Sk. Init.: Place hands on the mat in the cartwheel position and press the shoulders as the legs are lifted overhead into the cartwheel (b and c). Finish in a scale position and balance (d and e); then lift the arms upward overhead as the body pivots on the supporting leg (f) and step into another low scale position (a). Place the hands once again on the mat and press (b) into the cartwheel. Land in the low scale. By following this scale with a

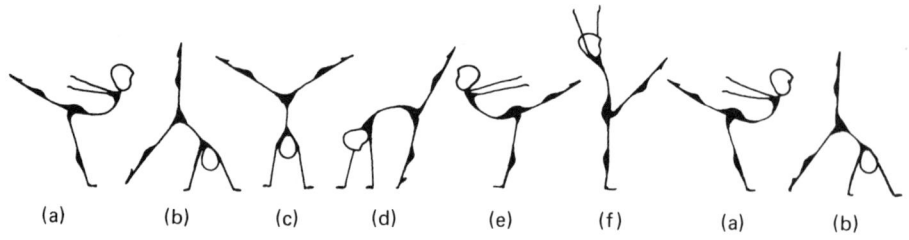

(a)　(b)　(c)　(d)　(e)　(f)　(a)　(b)

pivot and another scale, you will be working along the length of the mat while cartwheeling only on one side. You should return down the length of the mat by practicing this skill to the other side.

NEAR ARM CARTWHEEL
(One-arm cartwheel)

Execute the basic cartwheel, but use only one arm to support the body weight. Extend the other arm toward the ceiling during the skill. As a progression, use the cartwheel keeping the hands together (page 123).

The near arm is the first arm to contact the mat when doing a basic cartwheel. (If cartwheeling to the right side, the right arm is the first to contact the mat; since it is closer to the starting position of the body, it is referred to as the near arm. If cartwheeling to the left, the left arm is the near arm.)

The near arm cartwheel is the easiest one-arm cartwheel variation to begin, but it is difficult to land in a standing position. Bring the first leg to contact the mat in close to the supporting hand (d and e); if this leg is placed too far from the hand, you will fall because the base will not be under the center of gravity when the hand is lifted from the mat. Near arm cartwheels should be practiced to both the right and left sides.

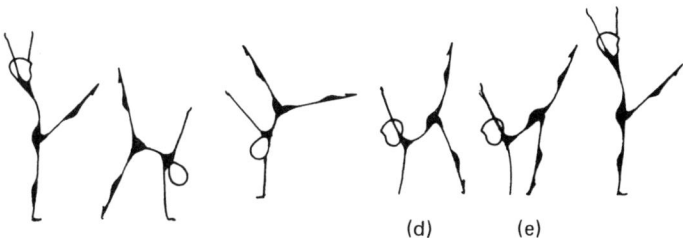

(d)   (e)

Variation:
Execute continuous near arm cartwheels alternating right

and left sides. See page 121 for directions but use only the near arm for each cartwheel. This alternation takes concentration.

FAR ARM CARTWHEEL
(One-arm cartwheel)

The far arm is the second arm to support the body weight in the basic cartwheel. This skill is somewhat frightening for the beginner to start because the supporting arm is on the far side of the head when going into the cartwheel. The landing is, however, much easier than that of the near arm cartwheel.

Execute continuous cartwheels down the length of the mat. Use only the far arm to support the body weight. Extend the free arm toward the ceiling. Practice the series on both the dominant and nondominant sides.

Variation:

Practice continuous far arm cartwheels alternating right and left sides (see page 121 for directions). Extend the free arm toward the ceiling and extend the supporting shoulder. Move slowly in a controlled manner as you alternate the cartwheels; move smoothly along the length of the mat.

CABRIOLE CARTWHEEL

Execute the basic continuous cartwheels to the straddled handstand position (b); *quickly* join the legs together (c) and then return to the straddled position (d) before finishing the cartwheel (e and f). Practice this series in a continuous manner to the dominant and the nondominant sides. There is a momentary stop in each handstand position while the leg action takes place.

Variation:

Execute continuous cabriole cartwheels alternating right and left sides (see page 121 for directions).

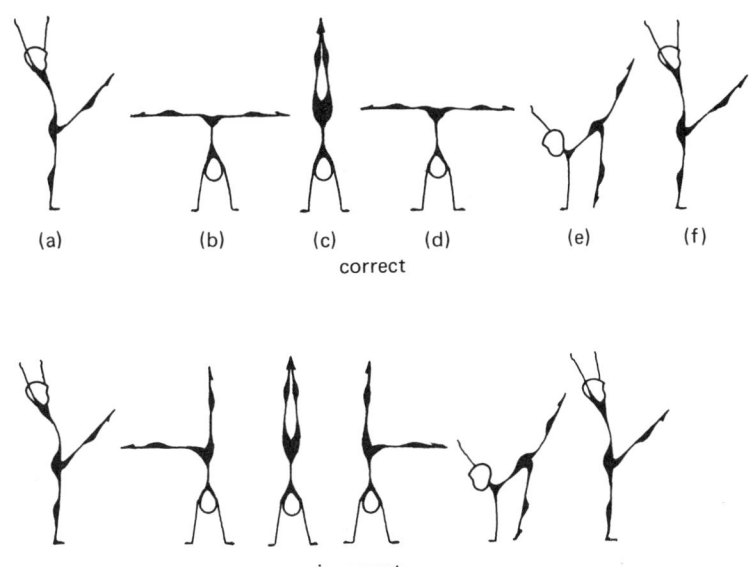

EUROPEAN TUMBLING SKIP INTO CARTWHEEL

Proceed as follows for a cartwheel to the *right side* (reverse directions for a left side cartwheel): Step (a) forward onto the left leg (b); hop on the left leg as the right leg is stretched obliquely backward; lift arms obliquely forward and upward; keep head up (c). As the arms reach down to the mat, quickly swing the right leg forward (d), step onto it (e), and execute the cartwheel to the right side. Practice this step, hop, and reach into a cartwheel several times. (As students learn to use this European tumbling skip into the cartwheel, then take several walking steps into the tumbling skip. To go to the right they would begin walking left, right, left. Then they would hop on the left and swing right forward into the cartwheel. As they learn to extend the leg backward and reach forward during the walk into the tumbling skip, have them increase the speed of the walk to a slow run.)

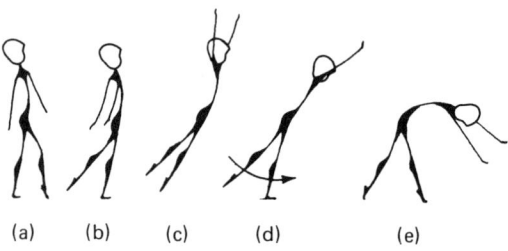

(a)   (b)   (c)   (d)   (e)

Since this will be a different style of tumbling skip for most students, it will take time for them to reprogram their minds to extend the free leg behind them rather than lift the knee to the chest as they are probably used to doing. The head and chest should lift upward during the hop, and the arms reach slightly forward and upward as the free leg reaches slightly backward and upward.

DIVING CARTWHEEL

Execute a running cartwheel with the European tumbling skip as explained on the previous page, but use a different pattern for the arm movement. During the hop, lift the arms and head (a); as the leg swings forward to go into the cartwheel, circle the arms backward by the ears (b) toward the hips (c); then reach vigorously forward and upward as you jump off the right leg thrusting the body into the air (d). The body drops to the mat on the hands (e) and the cartwheeling action is completed. In order to dive correctly into this cartwheel, you must concentrate on going high into the air, not covering horizontal distance. The high dive is accomplished by a blocking action of the right leg (for the right side cartwheel), the elevated position of the head and chest, and the proper timing of the arm thrust.

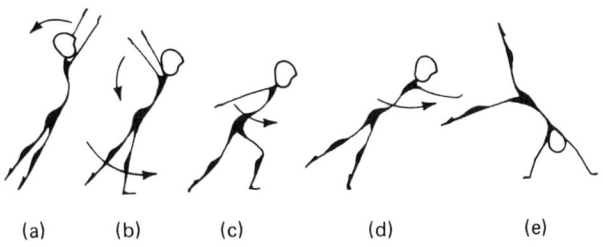

(a) (b) (c) (d) (e)

Variation:

The arm circle going into the diving cartwheel can be reversed. Reach forward and upward during the tumbling skip; then lower the arm forward past the hips, backward, and upward overhead as the dive takes place; you will land in the usual handstand position.

**CARTWHEEL TO KNEELING POSITION
(Far leg bends)**

Execute the basic cartwheel to the right. As the left leg contacts the mat, bend the knee (d) and lower the right knee to the mat (e). Kneel on the right knee with the left foot on the mat (e). Hold a pose position or lower the hips backward to the mat behind the right knee (f) and go into a backward roll (g) or after lowering the hips to the mat, kick the left leg in a straddle to the left side as (h–i). The right leg straightens (j) and follows;

Turn the body to the left as the left knee bends and kneel (k) onto this knee. Then step forward (l) onto the right foot to a stand on the right.

CARTWHEEL TO KNEELING POSITION ON NEAR LEG

Execute the basic cartwheel to the *right;* as the left leg is lowered to the mat, press with the shoulders to maintain most of the body weight. Place the left toes on the mat (d) as that knee quickly bends (e) and is lowered to the mat (f). Extend the right leg in the air as the arms press off the mat. Reach overhead and

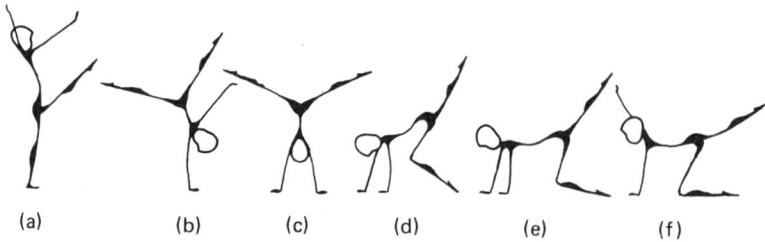

(g)　　　(h)　　(i)

turn the body to the right (g). Then place the right foot on the mat to stand (h) and turn on the right leg (i). This cartwheeling action must be slow in order to control the landing on the knee.

Variations:

  1. As the left knee is lowered to the mat, sit on that heel and lower the right leg to a half split position.

  2. As the left knee is lowered to the mat, place the hips on the mat behind the left foot and the hands on the mat near the hips. Swing the right leg up and to the right as the body turns to the right; extend the left leg to follow the right leg; bend the right leg and place the knee on mat so that you can kneel up onto the right knee. Then stand by stepping forward onto the left foot.

CARTWHEEL FROM KNEELING POSITION ON FAR KNEE

St. Pos.: Kneel on the left knee with the right foot on the mat so that you are ready to go into a *right side* cartwheel (a).

Sk. Init.: Lower the hands to the mat as the left leg is extended to begin the kick into the cartwheel (b); straighten the right leg to support the weight as the shoulders push and move the body into the cartwheel (c). Finish in any of the cartwheel variations.

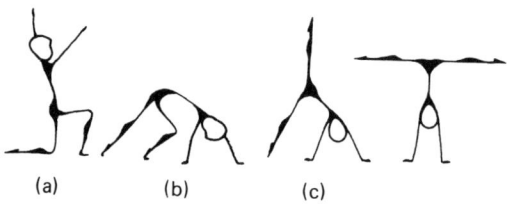

(a) (b) (c)

CARTWHEEL FROM KNEELING POSITION ON NEAR KNEE

St. Pos.: Kneel on the right knee with the left leg extended backward and the toes on the mat (a).

Sk. Init.: Lean the torso forward and place the hands on the mat as the left leg is lifted into the cartwheel action (b). Thrust the right leg into the cartwheel by straightening so that the weight is supported on the top of the toes (c). Then kick the leg into the basic cartwheel (d). Land in any of the variations. This skill takes a great deal of pressing action from the shoulders to move the hips into the cartwheel position.

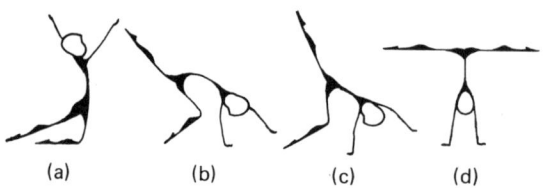

(a) (b) (c) (d)

cartwheels

ROUND-OFF

Progression:

1. Execute a slow cartwheel to a handstand position. Quickly join the legs together and then pike them down to the mat. The legs should be placed together during the handstand, not joined together just before the landing. Bend the knees only slightly upon landing.

2. Execute the European tumbling skip into the round-off progression as explained above.

3. Hop into the round-off progression and jump out of it: Execute progression (2), but force the shoulders to give a vigorous thrust off the mat as the legs pike downward. Upon landing, straighten the legs powerfully so that a rebounding jump is executed. The arms are overhead but slightly forward during the jump and the legs are pressed firmly together.

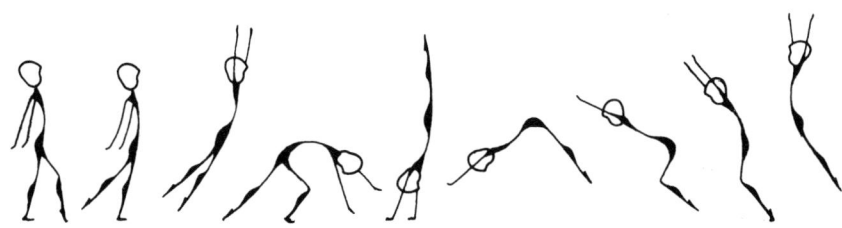

4. Take three or four walking steps into progression (3). As you learn the timing of this progression, change the walking steps into running steps. Notice that the body is momentarily suspended in the air after the arm thrust. The arm pattern is as explained for the handstand snap-down on page 67. This arm pattern and the rebounding jump are the most important phases of this skill.

Variations:

1. The body position out of the round-off during the rebounding jump can be changed to that of a straddle; stag; double

cartwheels

stag; split; split with the back leg bent so that the foot is to the head; arch jump with the knees bent and both feet to the head. The arm position for any of the jumps can also vary.

2. A one-quarter or one-half turn can take place during the rebounding jump as any one of the body positions listed above is used.

3. Any backward roll variation can follow the rebounding jump.

4. Any cartwheel variation can follow the one-half turning rebounding jump.

5. Any variation of the backward handspring can be used instead of the rebounding jump.

SWITCH LEG CARTWHEEL

St. Pos.: Stand ready to kick into a cartwheel to either the right or the left side (a).

Sk. Init.: Kick the rear leg upward into the handstand position and stay there (b) while the forward leg follows, passes by the extended leg (c), and then steps downward (d) as the arms press off the mat and lift overhead (e). Now face the opposite direction. (If the student cartwheels to the right side, the left leg kicks up into a handstand position and stays there as the right leg kicks up, brushes past the left leg, and then steps downward. The left leg follows. The student is now facing inward with the right leg forward.) Practice this skill on both the dominant and nondominant sides.

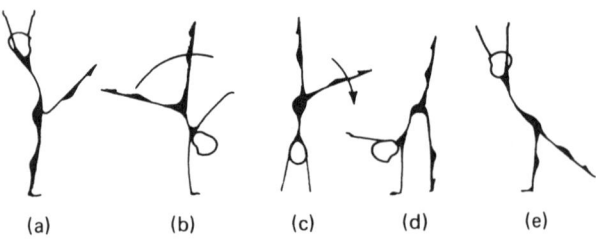

(a)   (b)   (c)   (d)   (e)

Variations:

Left and right side switch leg cartwheels can be alternated moving down the length of the mat by finishing one cartwheel, pivoting, and then stepping into the opposite side cartwheel. This too is followed by a pivot and another cartwheel. The kicking leg should pass directly next to the extended leg during each cartwheel so that the body is in the vertical plane.

SWING-THROUGH CARTWHEEL

Progression: Switch leg cartwheel (page 136).

St. Pos.:   If you usually cartwheel to the right side, proceed as follows (reverse for the dominant left side): Put the legs in position for a right side cartwheel; set the arms for a left side cartwheel (a).

Sk. Init.:   Lead the upper body into a left side cartwheel by kicking the left leg upward into the handstand position where it stays (b). Kick the right leg up fast, pass it by the left leg (c), and then step downward to the mat (d). Then lower the left leg to the mat through a cartwheeling action as the arms press off and reach overhead. Keep the back straight during this skill. Move all parts of the body through *only* the vertical plane. Practice this skill with the starting position reversed.

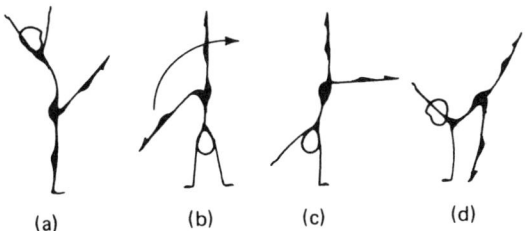

(a)   (b)   (c)   (d)

Variations:

1. Practice this swing-through cartwheel on a straight line to facilitate moving the skill onto the balance beam.

2. After the swing-through cartwheels have been learned on both the right and left sides, begin work on continuous swing-through cartwheels. As one cartwheel is finished, pivot as the first foot contacts the mat, the arms press off the mat, reach overhead, and change positions. Then step into the next swing-through cartwheel to the other side. Progress smoothly down the length of the mat. Maintain a very straight back.

3. Once variation (2) is learned, begin work on one arm swing-through cartwheels using the near arm on both the dominant and nondominant sides.

4. You can also execute one arm swing-through cartwheels on the far arm, but they are more difficult than on the near arm.

5. To execute a swing-through cartwheel to split, start with the right leg forward for a right split. It is important that the skill is executed through the vertical plane only.

QUARTER TURNING CARTWHEEL

Progression: Switch leg cartwheel (page 136).

St. Pos.: Be ready to execute a cartwheel to the right side [reverse for a left side cartwheel (a)].

Sk. Init.: Cartwheel to the handstand position (the legs are together by the time the left hand contacts the mat) (c). Immediately thrust the right arm off the mat to initiate a one-quarter turn (d) and reposition it next to the left hand in an English handstand (e). Hold the balance momentarily, and then open the legs to a split handstand position (f) so that the right leg when lowered will be the first leg to contact the mat (g).

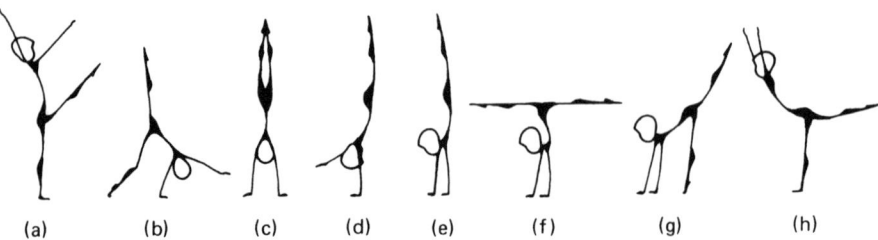

(a) (b) (c) (d) (e) (f) (g) (h)

cartwheels

Practice this skill on both the dominant and nondominant sides. Since the skill can be executed on the balance beam, you should be able to complete the entire skill on a straight line drawn down the center of the mat.

Variations:

1. Continuous quarter turning cartwheels to the right side: As the right leg steps down to the mat from the first quarter turning cartwheel, thrust the arms off the mat and reach overhead while executing a pivot to the left on the right leg; lift the right leg forward and upward and then replace it on the mat to begin the next quarter turning cartwheel. Reverse to execute the continuous action to the left side.

2. Continuous quarter turning cartwheels alternating right and left sides: At the completion of the right side quarter turning cartwheel execute a pivot to the left on the right leg [as in variation (1)]; lift the left leg upward and then replace it on the mat as you kick into a left side quarter turning cartwheel. Continue alternating left and right side quarter turning cartwheels down the length of the mat.

CARTWHEEL TO SPLIT

In order to land in a split with the right leg forward, a cartwheel to the left side must be executed.

Execute a slow cartwheel to the left side. Keep the body weight supported on the arms (a–c). Instead of touching the right foot to the mat to assume the standing position, pull the right leg forward (d–g) and drop the body into the split position with the hips next to the right hand (h).

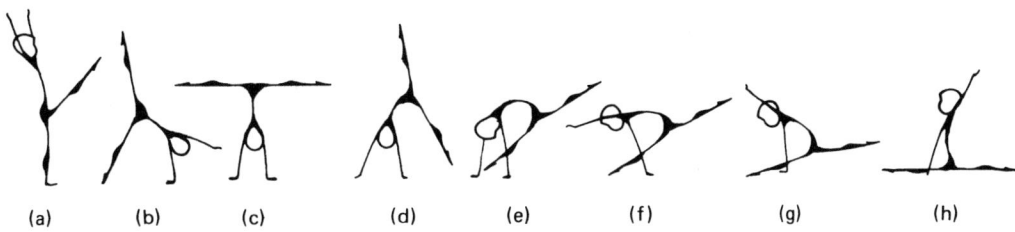

(a)　　(b)　　(c)　　(d)　　(e)　　(f)　　(g)　　(h)

Spotting: Stand facing the student's back. Give verbal cues to execute a *slow* cartwheel. Grasp the thigh area while the student is in the straddled handstand position. To assist in getting the student down to the right leg forward split, use your left hand on the *back* of the right thigh, pull it downward as for a cartwheel, but lift it upward slightly to slide past the hand position. Meanwhile, your right hand on the top of the left thigh is keeping the left leg in the vertical plane, and the left hand remains in place lowering the student gently to the mat into the split position.

PARTNER ONE-ARM CARTWHEELS

Progression: Practice continuous near arm and far arm cartwheels. Keep the free arm perpendicular to the body and parallel to the mat as if holding onto a partner.

The spotter can now face the student and hold onto the free arm while the student executes one-arm cartwheels. This is merely a safety check to see that the student is passing through the vertical plane and will not kick the partner.

St. Pos.: For near arm cartwheels partners face each other and hold each other's far hand. They then execute a series of near arm cartwheels (one partner cartwheels to the right side as the other cartwheels to the left side).

For far arm cartwheels partners face each other and hold each other's near hand. They then execute a series of far arm cartwheels continuously down the length of the mat. (They will now have to reach over their grasped hands to go into the cartwheel.)

Variation:

If one partner can execute only a near arm cartwheel correctly and the other can only execute a far arm cartwheel correctly, this skill can still be managed. Now the partners face each other and hold onto hands so that they are grasping right hands (or

cartwheels

left hands) only. The cartwheels are executed in a continuous manner.

CARTWHEEL ON CANE OR BATON

Progression: Continuous near arm cartwheels (page 127).

St. Pos.:   To execute a cartwheel to the right side, hold onto the cane or baton in the following manner: place the right hand near the base of the cane (baton); place the left hand about half way up the cane (baton). Keep the right arm straight during the cartwheel (just as if doing a near arm cartwheel on the right arm); keep the left arm bent to stabilize the cane (baton).

HALF TURNING CARTWHEELS

Execute a slow cartwheel on the right side to the straddled handstand position (a–c). Once the handstand position is reached, press the right arm off the mat (d), pivot the body over the left arm (e), and swing the right arm across the chest to help initiate the turning action. Then place the right arm to the other side of the left arm in another handstand position (f). Keep the legs straddled during the pivot and then continue the cartwheel action by having the right leg step down and then the left leg step down (g).

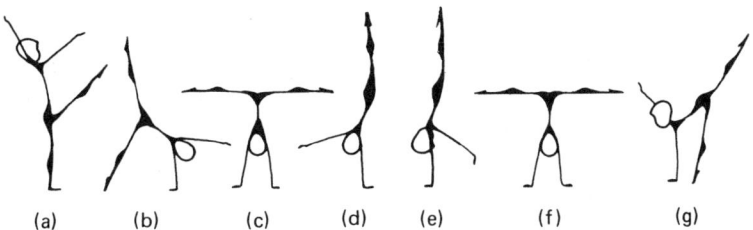

(a)   (b)   (c)   (d)   (e)   (f)   (g)

RUNNING QUARTER TURNING CARTWHEEL

St. Pos.: Start as for a running cartwheel with a European tumbling skip.

Sk. Init.: Kick the legs as the hands are placed on the mat (similar to the running cartwheel), but as soon as the hands contact the mat, join the legs together and thrust the arms off the mat to force the body into the air and into a one-quarter turn. The body lands in a handstand position followed by a step down action with the right leg in the lead if you started a right side cartwheel from the run. Since this skill moves rather quickly, the body must be balanced as the one-quarter turn is executed as in (b) and (c). (The legs do not kick upward with much force.)

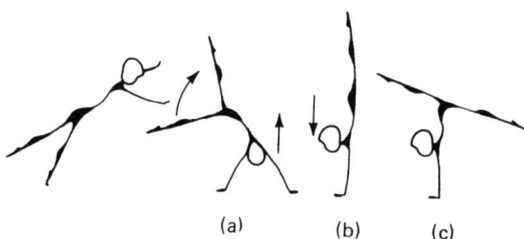

(a)   (b)   (c)

BUTTERFLY

This cartwheeling action is executed completely in the air with the body moving in a plane parallel to the mat.

Progression: You can walk through this move by starting in a straddle stand and piking forward at the hips. To go to the right side, "wind-up" by swinging the torso to the left, keeping the torso parallel to the mat. The torso then swings to the right by lowering the chest slightly toward the mat as the knees bend; then lift the chest and arms forcefully to a position parallel to the mat as the left leg is kicked backward, upward, and toward

cartwheels

the right. Keep parallel to the mat. Step downward with the left leg. As the right leg is kicked backward and upward forcefully toward the left, the body ends spinning on the left leg.

(Walk through this progression several times with the class. Watch for correct leg kicking technique. The legs must kick straight backward and then to the side.)

Sk. Init.: Execute this skill by piking forward and winding up to the left. Then as the body swings to the right, kick the left leg forcefully backward and upward as the right leg jumps and kicks backward and upward. The body spins in a stretched straddle position parallel to the mat. In order to get a powerful jump and kick into the skill, bend the knees into the wind-up action and then again during the thrusting action of the chest and arms. By executing this skill in a continuous series, you will move in a circular pattern on the mat.

FORWARD TINSICA

Progressions: Cartwheel; walkover (page 83).

St. Pos.: Begin as if starting a cartwheel to the dominant side. Place the hands on the mat for the cartwheel, but point the fingers toward the direction of the skill, not perpendicularly to the skill, as done for a cartwheel.

Sk. Init.: As the hands are placed on the mat one at a time, hold the shoulders at an oblique angle to the direction of the movement of this skill; the hips maintain this oblique angle as one leg followed by the other contacts the mat. The placement of the hands and the feet are on a straight line as if the skill is being done on the balance beam. There is a smooth rhythm to this skill with an even count of hand, hand, leg, leg. Keep the arms straight with the shoulders extended; also keep the legs straight.

Practice this skill on the nondominant side.

Variations:

The following variations can be used with the tinsica: kick, double kick, cabriole, spotters, gainers, swing-throughs, and walkover to split. (See Chapter 3 for directions.)

BACKWARD TINSICA

Progressions: Cartwheel; backward walkover (page 96).

St. Pos.: For a dominant left side, stand in a forward stride position with the left leg forward, weight on the right leg, arms overhead with the left arm slightly forward.

Sk. Init.: Keeping the hips at an oblique angle, arch backward extending the right shoulder; place that hand on the mat as the left leg kicks upward. The body passes over this right shoulder as the left hand is placed on the mat. The right leg jumps upward passing over both hands. The left leg lands followed by the right. Practice this skill on a straight line as if working on the balance beam. The backward tinsica has a smooth even rhythm like the cartwheel and the forward tinsica. The shoulders must be extended to maintain this even rhythm.

Practice this skill on the nondominant side.

Variations:

1. The following backward walkover variations can also be used with the backward tinsica: kick, double kick, cabriole, scissors, spotters, gainers, swing-throughs, and walkover to split. (See Chapter 3 for directions.)

cartwheels

2. Backward Tinsica to Handstand Balance: Initiate the basic backward tinsica as explained above (a and b). As the second hand contacts the mat and the legs reach the inverted split position (c), rotate the hips to assume the handstand balance with the legs straddled (d). At this point, join the legs together in a stretched handstand (e). Recovery can be made through any walkover (forward/backward) or forward limber variation.

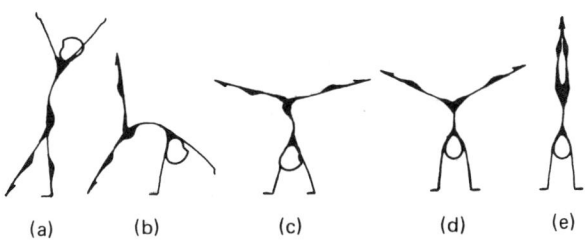

(a)　(b)　(c)　(d)　(e)

BACKWARD TINSICA WITH ONE-QUARTER TURN

St. Pos.: Stand ready to go into a backward tinsica on the non-dominant side (a).

Sk. Init.: Lean backward and place the first hand (b) and then the second hand on the mat (c). Lift the legs into the split handstand position with the shoulders and hips held at an oblique angle to the mat. Before stepping down out of this backward tinsica, rotate the hips so that the back will arch (d) (the hands have not moved) and you will end the skill by doing a forward tinsica (e) progressing in a straight line.

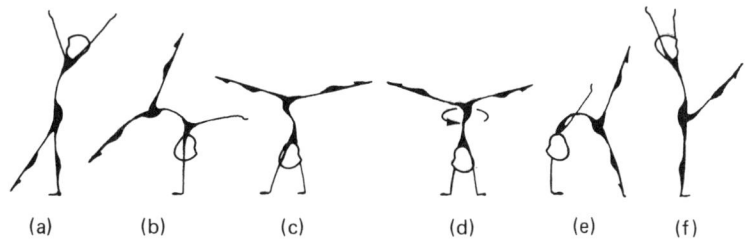

(a)　(b)　(c)　(d)　(e)　(f)

Variations:

1. If you prefer to start on the dominant side for the backward tinsica, the forward tinsica ending will occur on the non-dominant leg. If this is difficult, you can execute a scissoring action of the legs so that you will land once again on the dominant leg.

2. You can finish in a split position by bending the landing leg and placing the pointed toe followed by the knee as the hands thrust off the mat. Then drop the body into the split position.

ADDITIONAL CARTWHEEL VARIATIONS

ADDITIONAL CARTWHEEL VARIATIONS

5
springs

KNIP-UP PROGRESSION

    1. Assume the position in (a): extend the legs at a 45° angle with the horizontal, place the hands under the shoulders with the elbows pointing toward the ceiling, and keep the hips high above the mat—not low as in (b). (If the student is to spring high into the air, the hips must be in an elevated position above the mat. The hips should not be close to the mat. Briefly explain to the students the cues to this important position: legs extended at a 45° angle, hands under the shoulders with elbows pointing toward the ceiling, hips held high, weight supported on the back of the shoulders, head, and hand.)

correct   incorrect

(a)   (b)

springs

2. Starting from a squat position with the hands by the shoulders roll backward into the position illustrated in (a). Repeat this progression several times in order to learn to roll immediately to the desired stretched pike position with the hips elevated above the mat.

3. Assume the position in (a) below, and practice building up the momentum for the skill by taking a small downward beat with the legs (b), keeping the hips high (do not allow the feet to touch the mat). Using this beat to put the muscles under stretch, immediately thrust the legs upward and forward extending the body as in (c). The hips remain high, and the back arches as the legs begin downward (d). Bend knees and place the feet under the hips as in (e). (This progression was developed to give the student the kinesthetic feeling of the leg thrust and hip lift phase needed to execute a high knip-up.) Do not attempt to stand from this progression. Instead, land in either the position in (e) or in the back bend position in (f).

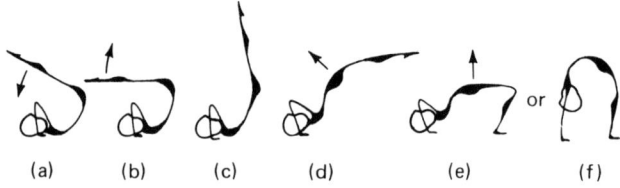

(a) (b) (c) (d) (e) (f)

Repeat this progression starting from a squatting position and rolling backward to the (a) position.

KNIP-UP

Using spotters, execute progression (3) above, but as the legs and hips extend forward and upward (c), push the head and arms off the mat (d) and swing the arms up and overhead and then forward (e and f). If the hips remain high, you will finish in a standing position with your arms overhead; if the hips drop, you will finish in a squatting position with your arms reaching forward parallel to the mat (g).

springs

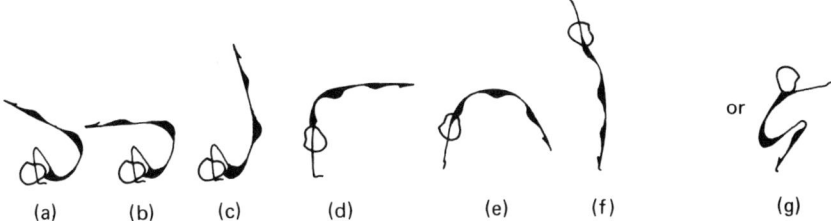

(a)   (b)   (c)   (d)   (e)   (f)   (g)

Spotting: Kneel on the left knee facing the right shoulder area of the student (a and b). Place the left hand on the student's right bicep (not the tricep) and grip firmly. (With this grip even if you lose the grip, the student's bent elbow locks your hand in a position where it is still possible to lift.) Place the right arm under the upper back so that during the leg thrust and extension phase you will be able to lift the student's upper body into the standing position.

Note: Be sure that students have successfully executed progression (3) so that their timing will be correct. If they do not time their efforts correctly, they may do a back extended roll and unless the spotters are alert, they will not be able to help the student.

Variations:
    1. Once the basic skill is learned, practice thrusting the hips higher so that it will be possible to land in a lay-out position.
    2. Finish in a step-out position.
    3. During the leg thrust and arm extension initiate a one-half turn stepping down one leg at a time.

Note: Since this is a spring, the body is momentarily suspended in the air before the landing.

HEADSPRING PROGRESSION

St. Pos.: Assume starting position (a) with the hands near the face (not in the usual headstand position), hips held high, and the forehead at hairline area contacting the mat.

Sk. Init.: From this position give a small jump extending the legs, forcing the hips overhead, and keeping the toes close to the mat (b and c). (Students tend to lift the legs to a position parallel to the mat (d) which will cause a low springing action. Spotters can prevent this error by giving verbal cues and manually moving the hips into position keeping the legs low.)

Spotting: Two spotters kneel to each side of the student's shoulder area. For this progression, they place the near arm around the small of the student's back and the far hand on the back of the near thigh. They now have the leverage necessary to move the hips over the student's head and can notice if the feet are being held close to the mat. Once the hips pass into position, the spotters cue the student that it would be time to throw the legs *if* they were doing the entire skill. Students should practice getting into this position several times with the help of spotters and listening for the cue to execute the leg thrust.

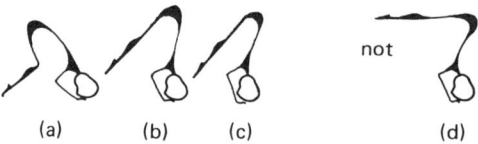

(a)　(b)　(c)　　　　(d)

HEADSPRING

St. Pos.: Assume starting position (a).

Sk. Init.: With the help of the spotters and with a slight jump the hips pass through position (b) to position (c). Once the hips are overhead, begin the upward and forward leg thrust (d). As the legs thrust, extend the body and thrust the arms off the mat (e). Keep the hips high as the legs return to the mat (e), the arms swing up overhead, then forward quickly and land in a semi-squat position (f and g).

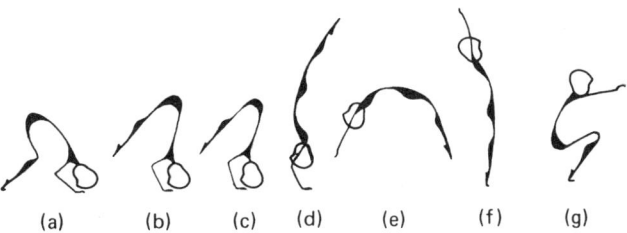

(a) (b) (c) (d) (e) (f) (g)

Spotting: The spotters assist as in the progression until they are sure that the hips are passing over the student's head. At that time the spotters move their hands from the thigh area to a position grasping the student's bicep. Once they have a firm grip, they tell the student to execute the leg thrust and then they assist in lifting the upper body to the semi-squat position.

Variations:

As you are learning this skill, you can get higher if you execute the leg thrust and arm extension before the hips pass beyond the head position. As you learn to extend the hips upward, you can land in any of the following positions:

1. Lay-out.
2. Step-out.
3. Straddle Sitting Position: Execute a high headspring. As the legs pass overhead, straddle them (c) and lower the feet to the mat forward of the hips in the straddle position (d). First the toes, then the heels, and then the hips contact the mat (e). As the hips contact the mat, pike the head and chest forward to absorb the force of the landing (f).

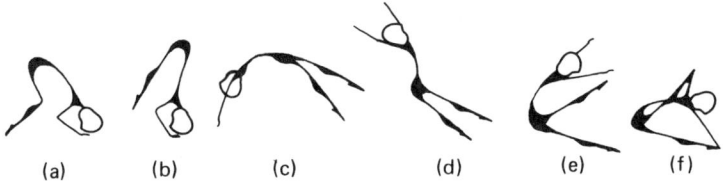

(a) (b) (c) (d) (e) (f)

4. Pike Sitting Position: Use the above technique and keep the legs together and straight. First the toes and then the heels

contact the mat. As the hips are lowered to the mat, pike the upper body forward and lower the head to the knees.

5. Kneeling Position: Execute a high headspring as if landing in a lay-out position. Just before landing arch the back, bend the knees, and pull the feet toward the head so that the pointed toes and insteps contact the mat slightly before the knees. Use spotting directions for the basic headspring. Lift the student high enough to land in the stretched kneeling position. Maintain your grip on the student's arm to stabilize the kneeling position or the student may fall forward.

6. Split Position: Execute a high headspring. As the legs pass overhead, separate them, shove the hands off the mat, and initiate a one-quarter twist toward the desired forward split leg. Land in a stride split position crosswise on the mat.

FORWARD HANDSPRING PROGRESSION

Progression: Handstand (page 62); front limber (page 79); and the following exercises:

1. Tumbling Skip into Handstand: Take one step into the tumbling skip; then step into the handstand. (Spotters stop the student from kicking past or arching over from the handstand position.) Do not attempt to hold this handstand; merely learn to kick to it quickly after executing the tumbling skip. Extend the shoulders by the time the hands contact the mat.

2. Take several steps into the tumbling skip to the handstand. (Once again the spotters stop the momentum in the handstand position and then have the student step down.) As you work on this progression, increase the speed to a gentle run to give the feeling of the speed needed for the handspring.

3. Handspring approach as described above with the shoulder thrust: As soon as the hands contact the mat going into the handstand, thrust the shoulders and arms off the mat. (The spotters grasp the near thigh and assist by lifting upward as the student initiates the shoulder thrust. The student is replaced gently into the handstand position by the two spotters.) Do not bend the elbows for the progression; merely begin to extend the shoulders just before the hands contact the mat.

FORWARD HANDSPRING

Once the progressions as explained above have been practiced, continue with the entire skill. Make use of the spotters.

Spotting: The spotters kneel on one or both knees facing each other and have the student place the hands on the mat in the area indicated by the "X."

springs

As the student approaches, she should be cued to kick the heels forcefully and thrust off the mat with the arms and shoulders. As the hands are placed on the mat, the spotter grasps the upper arm and places her other arm around the student's upper back near the shoulder area. As the student shoves off the mat, the spotters lift her arms and upper body into a semi-squat ending position, maintaining their grasp on the upper arm to help absorb the momentum of the spring.

Note: This is an easy skill to spot if the students have previously worked on the progressions. The class can be divided into groups of three or more to practice while rotating in as spotters.

Variations:

After learning the basic front handspring, land in any of the following positions:

1. Lay-out.
2. Step-out.
3. Straddle Sitting Position: Use the same technique as used in the headspring to the straddle seat (page 153). (Basic handspring spotting is used to lift the student's hips high enough to allow the feet to contact the mat before the hips are lowered to the sitting position.)
4. Pike Sitting Position: Use the same technique as used in (3). Keep the legs together and straight. Arch the back and point the toes so that the feet contact the mat before the hips drop to the mat. As the hips contact the mat, lower the chest to the knees to absorb the force of the landing.
5. One-Arm Handspring: Use the same technique as used in the basic forward handspring. Lift both arms overhead during the tumbling skip. Place only one on the mat. Swing the other through the handstand position to finish overhead for the lay-out or step-out or to a position reaching forward parallel to the mat for the squat ending. Do not bend the supporting arm.
6. On Baton or Cane: After practicing the one arm handspring, use that supporting hand to grasp close to the base of the baton or cane. The other hand grasps just above the midsection of the baton. The implement is held crosswise in front of the body. Using the running three-step approach with the tumbling skip, reach out and place the base of the baton on the mat while

holding it steady with the other arm (elbow is bent) and kick over into the handspring. You must push off the mat with the baton and lift it over the head and then forward just as the arms are used in the basic handspring.

7. Cabriole: Execute the basic handspring step-out but join the legs together during the handstand phase using a cabriole beat (the legs are rotated outward at the hip and slightly crossed so that when they beat together the legs contact each other at the calf area). This beat is quick. Merely clap the legs together and then open to the stride position to complete the handspring step-out.

8. Scissors Handspring: This is similar to the basic handspring step-out, but thrust the arms off the mat as the legs kick to the opposite split position. Follow this change by the step-out. (Students may prefer to execute the tumbling skip and the beginning of the handspring on the nondominant leg so that after the scissor action the landing will take place on the dominant leg.)

9. Half Twisting Handspring: Begin the skill as if doing the basic handspring to a lay-out position, but do not kick as hard (delay the leg action somewhat). As soon as the hands contact the mat, they thrust off and initiate a one-half twist (meanwhile the legs have been joined together), and the hands then land on the mat again in a handstand position. (This skill moves very quickly. The handstand positions are not held, and the hands contact the mat only long enough to push off the mat.)

BACKWARD HANDSPRING PROGRESSION

1. Handstand, Snap-down, Rebounding Jump with Arm Throw: This progression is actually the last half of the back handspring and the movement into another back handspring. The push off from the arms and shoulders is most important, the arms should lead the head and chest upward during the snap-down action of the legs; the legs should be kept together during the rebounding jump. Kick into a handstand position (a and b) and then execute the shoulder thrust as the legs begin to snap downward (c). Suspend the body momentarily in the air as the arms lead the head and chest to an extended position (d and e); the legs prepare to

jump off the mat into a high rebounding jump before landing from the snap-down. During the rebounding jump (f) whip the arms overhead. Keep your arms close together; they should be no farther apart than shoulders width. (A cue might be to keep the arms by the ears.)

Practice this progression several times daily.

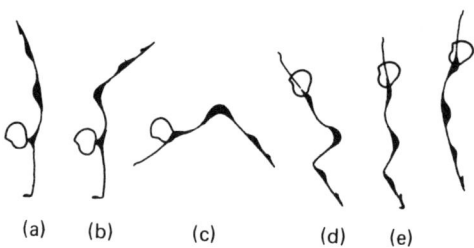

(a)   (b)   (c)   (d)   (e)

2. The Lean: Stand with the feet together and the legs straight, the arms extended overhead, and the feet flat on the mat (a). (Spotters stand on either side with one arm around the student's upper back. This arm is slightly bent, and rotated so that the elbow is held high on the student's back; the hand must be low enough to grasp the front side of the ribs in order to pull the student backward if necessary. The other hand is placed on the back of the student's near thigh.) Keeping the feet flat on the mat (the toes should not be lifted off the mat during this progression) and while keeping the back straight, lean backward into the spotters' arms (do not allow the back to arch) (b). [After the hips have moved beyond the base of the heels, the spotters return the student to the balanced standing position (a).] Repeat this leaning action several times so that you will learn to maintain a tight back and keep the feet flat on the mat while the arms are overhead and the head is held in a neutral position.

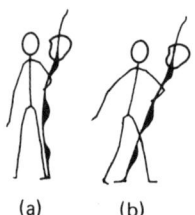

(a)   (b)

springs

3. Lean and Jump: Repeat the above progression (a and b) and add a backward and upward jump as the hips pass beyond the heels. Bend the knees slightly to initiate the jump (c and d). [Spotting is the same as for progression (2). The spotters hold the student during the leaning phase and maintain body balance during the jump phase. They try to help keep the student's back from arching by putting the high elbow around the student's back and by using the other hand to lift the thighs in the direction of the jump. The student is returned to the balanced starting position.] Repeat this lean and jump several times until you gain the kinesthetic awareness of this jumping position and the timing of the jump. (This must be done with spotters.)

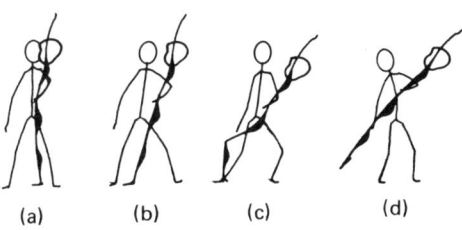

(a)   (b)   (c)   (d)

Once you have mastered the above progressions, it is time to combine the progressions into the complete backward handspring skill. You will need the assistance of the spotters.

LEAN-BACK BACKWARD HANDSPRING

The student's and spotters' starting position is as described in progression (3) above. The student leans backward; as the center of gravity moves past the heels, the student jumps backward looking back for the mat as the legs are lifted to the handstand position. The spotters allow the body to rotate by doing the following: The high elbow on the student's back is lowered during the jump to permit a slight arch; the hand on the thigh lifts the legs into the handstand position. From the handstand a snap-down followed immediately by a high rebounding jump is executed. The spotters merely position the hips and the legs to this handstand position; the arm on the student's back remains there in case the student allows the shoulders to fall forward. (If that occurs, the spotters continue to move the hips in the direction of the skill so that the student can step down onto the mat. If the shoulders stay in place during the handstand position, the spotter has nothing to do.) The spotter must not be tempted to throw the legs downward for the student, because the student must initiate this snapping action and the rebounding jump.

The rebounding jump out of the handspring is important because it gives the student the feeling of working out of this basic skill and into another skill. Once the student is successful in executing this progression with a minimum of spotting (spotters are needed with this starting position), the student moves on to the next skill.

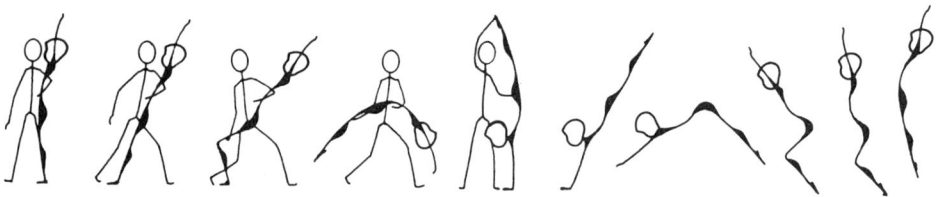

BACKWARD HANDSPRING FROM HANDSTAND SNAP-DOWN

This combination is similar to the handstand snap-down, high rebounding jump; the rebounding jump however, will be the take-off for the back handspring. Spotting this skill is easy, but the spotters must move fast and keep their faces out of the path of the arm swing (be sure to train the students to keep the arms by the ears!). The spotters can practice getting into position by spotting the rebounding jump out of a snap-down as the student warms up for this combination. During the handstand position the spotters are ready to move in to grasp around the student's back as soon as the snap-down action takes place. By the time the student begins to go into the jump the spotters should have an arm around the student's back and the other hand should be on the student's thigh. Once the spotters have practiced moving in to grasp the student for the handspring, move on to the entire skill by telling the student that she must pull her legs toward her hands during the snap-down and she must jump, traveling backward while throwing the arms and head back to the handstand position. Spot heavily during the first attempts. Remind the student to follow the handspring with another rebounding jump, reaching with arms towards the ceiling. This again gives the student the feeling of working into another skill.

With practice the student should be able to do this with only one and then no spotters. At this point she would be able to work on a series of back handsprings. As the student learns to rotate the body backward into the handstand position when lifting the legs, it is safe to spot her by using a belt or a couple of towels. Before the student learns the rotating action, the belt will jerk her into a back bend position. The spotters are left holding her body suspended by the belt in the air; then they would have to lower her to the mat in this back bend position. If a tumbling belt is not available, cut a slit lengthwise in a large towel so that the student can step into the center of the towel. The spotters hold onto the ends of the towel and move down the length of the mat with the tumbler. Since the towel is loose fitting, the tumbler is able to execute twisting movements, for example, the round-off, without getting tangled in the towel.

SIT-BACK, BACK HANDSPRING PROGRESSION

1. Handstand snap-down, high jump (page 67).
2. Sit-back, Whip-back with Spotter: The student stands with the legs and feet together, the arms by the sides, and the head up (a). The spotter stands directly behind the student ready to catch the student's back as the sit-back, whip-back action takes place. The spotter pushes the student from (b) back to (a), the starting position. As the student executes the sit-back, whip-back, notice that the torso maintains the upright position and that the arms have moved backward as indicated in (b). Students often resort to dropping the torso in order to maintain the balance (c). Jumping from this position will cause a very high back handspring which is undesirable. Jumping into the back handspring from (b) results in a lower, more powerful handspring.

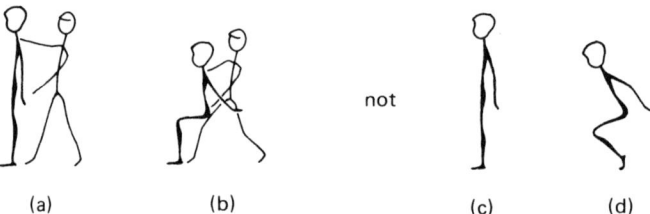

(a) (b) not (c) (d)

3. Sit-back, Whip-back, High Jump: The progression described above is repeated with the addition of a powerful backward and upward jump (c). The spotter now places one hand on the back of the student's neck and the other on the back just above the waistline (a). Using a lifting action, the spotter assists the student from (b) to (c) and then returns the student to the starting position (a).

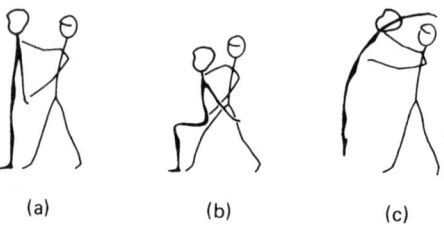

(a) (b) (c)

springs

SIT-BACK, BACK HANDSPRING

When the student learns the aforementioned progressions for the back handspring, the spotter moves to a position facing the student's side ready to assist in executing the total skill. During the sit-back phase the spotter places one arm around the small of the back; as the student begins the arm throwing action into the jump, the spotter places the free hand under the near thigh in order to insure that the legs will reach the handstand phase. During the handstand snap-down phase the spotter maintains contact with the small of the back as a safety precaution to control the student in case the shoulders fall forward of the hands. The arm on the back will move the center of gravity in the direction of the skill so that the student can land safely.

BACKWARD HANDSPRING VARIATIONS

1. Step-out: Execute the handspring to the handstand position; then open the legs to a split position and step down one leg at a time.

2. Step down from the handspring as above, but add a one-half turn as the first foot contacts the mat. Reach the arms *forcefully* overhead and take a step forward onto the second leg.

3. Back Handspring to Handstand Balance: Execute a high and rather slow take-off for the back handspring so that the backward momentum is absorbed in the handstand position. Press with the fingers and stretch the toes to the ceiling to help maintain balance.

4. Handspring to Headstand Balance: Use the same technique as in variation (3), but do not hold the handstand position.

Instead, pass through the handstand position and absorb the force. Then lower to a balanced headstand.

5. Handspring to Split: Using the same take-off as described in (3), do not attempt to hold the handstand but instead thrust quickly off the mat with the shoulders, getting the body high enough to pull the forward split leg through the position where the hands were. Drop into the split with the hips landing in the place where the hands were. (A spotter should help to lift the student high on the take-off.)

6. Backward Handspring to Chest Roll: Execute the take-off as described in (3). Do not hold the handstand, but bend the elbows and arch the back as the head is pulled through the arm position. By this time the chest contacts the mat, the feet are still high in the air, and you roll downward into a prone position; or by maintaining a tightly arched back you can kneel up into an extended position and then continue to maintain the arch. Execute a toe stand and finish in an erect standing position.

7. One-Arm Back Handspring: This can be practiced from a standing position or from a series of back handsprings. You should learn to do the skill on either arm and should practice alternating the arms when doing a series of one arm handsprings. The handspring technique is as usual with a great deal of shoulder thrust from the supporting arm.

8. Backward Forearm Handspring: Bend the elbows and grasp the wrist of the opposite arm. Maintain this grip and execute a backward forearm spring. (This is not a very asthetic move.)

9. Twisting Handspring: The basic handspring technique is used to the handstand position. Once this position is reached, thrust off; twist the hips vigorously to execute a one-half turn before landing in a squat position. Once this technique is mastered, practice getting higher so that a lay-out landing is possible after the one-half twist.

ADDITIONAL SPRING VARIATIONS

ADDITIONAL SPRING VARIATIONS

index

A

Acrobatics (*see* Back bends, variations)
Arabian limbers, 82, 111
Arab wheels (*see* Cartwheels; Tinsica)

B

Back bends, 73–116
  progressions, 73–77
    pose positions, 77
    push-up, 73
    rock, 74
    rock with arm thrust, 74–75
    rock with leg thrust, 76
    with spotting, 75
  variations, 77–116
    back bend skills, 77–79
      inside-outs, 78
      pony kicks, 79
      rotating, 77
      sideways, 77
      walking feet first, 77
      walking head first, 77
    limbers, 79–82, 111–12
      back Arabian, 111
      front limber, 79–82
    Veldez:
      progressions, 112–13
      to handstand, 113
    walkovers, backward, 96
      cabriole, 101
      on cane or baton, 104
      control, 99
      double kick, 101
      full turning, 110
      gaining, 105
      half turning, 109
      to handstand balance, 108
      kick, 100

Back bends (*continued*)
    kickover, 96
    one arm, 103
    partner, 107
    scissors, 102
    to split, 107
    spotting, 104
    to Swedish fall, 98
    swing-through, 106
  walkover, forward, 83
    cabriole, 87
    on cane or baton, 93
    chasing, 94
    control, 85
    double kick, 86
    double scissor, 89
    kick, 86
    one-arm, 91
    one-arm control, 92
    one-arm partner, 93
    partner, 89
    scissor, 88
    spotting, 95
    to split, 90
Back extended roll, 37–39 (*see also* Rolls, backward)
Backward roll, 29–41 (*see also* Rolls, backward)
Bridge, 73 (*see also* Back bends)
Butterfly, 142

C

Cabriole, 87, 101, 157
Cartwheels, 119–46
  progressions, 119–20
    handstand position, 119
    lunge position kick-over, 120
    switch kick, 119
  variations:
    Arab wheel, 143–46 (*see also* Tinsica)
    butterfly, 142
    cabriole, 128
    on cane or baton, 141
    continuous, 120
    continuous, alternating left and right sides, 121
    control, 125
      using scale position, 125
      using scale position progressing down length of mat, 126
    diving, 130
    European tumbling skip, 129
    far arm, 128
    from kneeling position, 134
      to half split, 133
      to straddle kick turn, 133
    full pivot into back roll, 124
    half turning, 141
    to inward lunge, 122
    to kneeling position on far leg, 131
    to kneeling position on near leg, 132
    to half split, 133
    to straddle kick turn, 133
    near arm, 127
    one-arm, 127–28 (*see also* Cartwheels, near and far arm)
    to outward lunge, 123
    partner one-arm, 140
    quarter turn, 138
      continuous, 139
      continuous, alternating right and left sides, 139
    round-off, 135
      progressions, 135
      variations, 135–36
    running, 129 (*see also* Cartwheels, European tumbling skip)
    running quarter turn, 142

Cartwheels (*continued*)
    to split, 139
    swing-through, 137
    switch leg, 136
    tinsica, backward, 144
        to handstand balance, 145
        variations, 144
    tinsica, backward with quarter turn, 145
        scissors, 146
        to split, 146
    tinsica, forward, 143
        variations, 144
    with hands held together, 123

D

Diving cartwheel, 130
Diving roll, 25

E

Elbow stand, 58–62 (*see also* Inverted balances, forearm)
European tumbling skip, 129

F

Flick-flack (*see* Springs, backward handsprings)
Flip-flop (*see* Springs, backward handsprings)
Flips (*see* Springs)
Forearm balance, 58–62 (*see also* Inverted balances, forearm)

G

Gaining walkovers, 105

H

Handstands, 62–69 (*see also* Inverted balances)
Head kip, 149–51 (*see also* Springs, headsprings)
Headstand, 55–58 (*see also* Inverted balances)

I

Inside-outs, 78
Inverted balances:
    elbow stand, 58–62
    extended tri-pod, 53
        variations, 54
    forearm, 58–62
        progression, 58
        variations:
            to backbend pose, 60
            to chest stand, 60
            elbow balance, 61
            to forward roll, 60
            hand-forearm balance, 61
            to knee scale, 59
            to limber, 60
            pose positions, 59
            walkover to split, 61
    handstand, 62–69
        poses, 64
        progressions:
            against wall, 63
            joining legs together, 62
            switch kick, 62
            with spotters, 62
            yogi, 63

Inverted balances (*continued*)
  variations into:
    cartwheel, 68
    half turn, 68
    kneeling position, 69
    press, 69
  variations out of:
    to backbend pose, 66
    to forearm balance, 66
    to forward roll, 66
    to headstand, 66
    jumping on hands, 68
    to kneeling position, 65
    to limber, 66
    to pike stand, 65
    pivot and roll, 68
    snap-down, 67
    to split, 66
    step down, 65
    to straddle L, 66
    to straddle stand, 65
    to straight arm forward roll, 66
    to Swedish fall, 65
    walking on hands, 67
    walking on hands with split kicks, 67
    to walkover, 66
  headstand, 55–58
    pose positions, 55
    progressions:
      extended tri-pod balance, 53
      tri-pod balance, 51
    variations:
      to forearm balance, 57
      to forward roll, 56
      to handstand, 57
      to knee scale, 56
      pose combinations, 55
      rotating, 56
      to straddle-down, 56
  tip-up, 53
    variations:
      control tip-up, 53
      to forward roll, 53
  tri-pod, 51
    variations:
      control, 52
      to forward roll, 52

J

Jumping in handstand balance, 68

K

Kick, 86
  double, 86
  pony, 79
  switch, 62, 119
Kip, 149–54 (*see also* Springs, knip-up)
Knip-up, 149–51 (*see also* Springs)

L

Limbers, 79–82, 111–12 (*see also* Back bends)

O

One-arm cartwheel, 127–28
One-arm handspring, 164
One-arm walkover, 91, 103

P

Pony kicks, 78

R

Rolls, 9–43
  backward, 29, 41
    progressions:
      pike position push-ups, 28
      roll back, feet down, 27
      roll back, feet down placing weight on feet, 28
    variations:
      back extended, 37 (see also Backward roll)
      to both knees, 31
      to chest stand, 40
      to forearm stand, 37
      to handstand, 37–39
      to headstand, 35
      to knee scale, 29
      to lunge, 33
      pike, 35
      to prone position, 32
      to stand, 29
      straddle, 33
      to wide arm handstand, 39
      without hands, 40
  forward, 9–27
    progressions, 7–9
      pike position push-ups, 8
      pike position push-ups with head tucked, 9
      tuck position roll-up, 7
      tuck position roll-up to stand, 8
    variations:
      to body wave, 21
      diving, 25
      to half split, 13
      to handstand balance, 23
      to jump, 20
      kick-back, 26
      to kneeling lunge position, 18
      to knee scale, 12
      to knee spin, 25
      to lunge, 19
      quarter turn to kneeling position, 17
      quarter turn to split, 16
      to split, 16
      to stand, 9
      straddle, 14
      straddle without hands, 23
      to supine position, 10
      without hands, 22
  side shoulder, 42, 43
    backward shoulder, 43
      to half split, 43
      to knee scale, 43
      to sitting pose, 43
    forward shoulder, 43
      to both knees, 43
      from kneeling position, 43
      to sitting pose, 43
    tuck position side roll, 42
      to kneeling lunge position, 42
      reverse direction, 42
      to sitting pose or half split, 42
      to stand, 43
Round-off, 135–36 (see also Cartwheels, variations)
Running cartwheel, 129 (see also European tumbling skip)

S

Scissors:
  backward walkover, 101–102, 106
  double, 89
  forward walkover, 88, 89
Shoulder roll, 43

Side roll, 42–43
Somersault (see Rolls)
Split, 16, 88, 107, 164
  half, 13, 30, 43
  straddle, 38
  stride, 34, 36
Spotting:
  backward walkover, 104
  forward walkover, 95
Springs, 149–64
  handsprings, 155–64
    backward handsprings, 157–64
      handstand, snap-down, backward handspring, 160
      handstand, snap-down, rebounding jump, 157
      lean-back, backward handspring, 159
      sit-back back handspring, 163
      sit-back back handspring progression, 162
      variations to the back handspring, 163–64
    forward handspring, 155–57
      progressions, 155
      variations, 156–57
  head kip, 151–54 (see also Headsprings)
  headsprings, 151–54
    progression, 151
    to semi-squat position, 152
    variations:
      to kneeling position, 154
      lay-out, 153
      to pike sitting position, 153
      to split, 154
      step-out, 153
      to straddle sitting position, 153

kip (see Knip-up)
knip-up, 149–51
  progression, 149
  to semi-squat position, 150
  variations:
    to half turn, 151
    lay-out, 151
    step-out, 151
  Neckspring, 149–51 (see also Knip-up)
Straddle, 14
  L, 38, 66
Swedish fall, 65, 98, 101

T

Tinsica:
  backward, 144–45
  backward with quarter turn, 145
  forward, 143
Tip-up, 53
Tri-pod, 51
  extended, 53
  (see also Inverted balances)

V

Veldez, 112–16 (see also Back bends)

W

Walkovers:
  backward, 96–112
  forward, 83–95